Wentworth Letter
Mormon 6:6

Mesomania

Plates / Alines 52:20
Alma 62:18
Alma 62:19

There's only one Cumorah.
And it's not in Mesoamerica!

Josiah Priest
Am. Antiquities

Mountains? Hel 10:9

Earthquakes!
3 Nephi: 8
New Madrid - Missouri

D&C 125 Zarahemla
(Sec. 18:1)

Mesomania

LDS NONFICTION BY JONATHAN NEVILLE

THE LOST CITY OF ZARAHEMLA

LETTER VII: OLIVER COWDERY'S MESSAGE TO THE WORLD ABOUT THE HILL CUMORAH

MORONI'S AMERICA

MORONI'S AMERICA (POCKET EDITION)

BROUGHT TO LIGHT

THE EDITORS: JOSEPH, WILLIAM, AND DON CARLOS SMITH

MORONI'S HISTORY (2016)

WEB:
www.moronisamerica.com/
www.lettervii.com/
bookofmormonwars.blogspot.com/
bookofmormonconsensus.blogspot.com

MESOMANIA

There's only one Cumorah.
And it's not in Mesoamerica!

Jonathan Neville, MS, JD

Mesomania

Mesomania: There's only one Cumorah, and it's not in Mesoamerica!
Copyright © 2016 by Jonathan Neville
All rights reserved.
First Edition, Second Printing
This is a work of nonfiction. The author has made every effort to be accurate and complete and welcomes comments, suggestions, and corrections, which can be emailed to lostzarahemla@gmail.com.

The opinions expressed in this work are the responsibility of the author alone.
9-12-16

ISBN-13: 978-1-944200-22-0

Front cover: Illustration by Catherwood

www.digitalegend.com

Mesomania

To open-minded people everywhere

NOTE TO READER: This book evaluates the historical and logical development of the theory that the Book of Mormon took place in Mesoamerica.

The author is a faithful, believing member of the Church of Jesus Christ of Latter-day Saints who accepts the Book of Mormon as an authentic record of an ancient people who lived in North America—not Mesoamerica. He also accepts the other canonized latter-day scriptures, as well as the Bible, as authoritative.

This is a condensed, introductory version of a longer work that contains more footnotes and citations omitted here in the interest of space. However, some notes are located at the end of the book.

Mesomania

132 *The Worlds of Joseph Smith*

A Page from John Lloyd Stephens, *Incidents of Travel in Central America, Chiapas, and Yucatan* (New York, 1841). John Bernhisel sent Joseph Smith a copy of this book. In his thank you letter, Joseph commented, "It unfolds & developes many things that are of great importance to this generation & corresponds with & supports the testimony of the Book of Mormon; I have read the volumes with the greatest interest." This impressive two-volume work was rich with etchings of buildings and monuments, such as this stela at Quirigua, Guatemala. Stephens' detailed observations led many early LDS leaders, including Parley P. Pratt, John Taylor, John E. Page, Orson Pratt, and George Q. Cannon, personally to consider Mesoamerica as the central area in the geography of the Book of Mormon.

Dean C. Jessee, ed. and comp., *Personal Writings of Joseph Smith* (1984; reprint, Salt Lake City: Deseret Book; Provo, Utah: Brigham Young University Press, 2002), *533. See also John L. Sorenson, *An Ancient American Setting for the Book of Mormon* (Salt Lake City: Deseret Book and Foundation for Ancient Research and Mormon Studies, 1985).

Part of the Exhibit from the Library of Congress event titled "The Worlds of Joseph Smith," held in Washington, D.C. in 2005. This is a page from the *BYU Studies* volume containing the proceedings.

Table of Contents

Opening Exercises 1
Huge Caveat – It's Okay to Have Different Ideas 3
Chapter 1 – The Year 2016 5
Chapter 2 – It's Okay to Discuss Geography 7
Chapter 3 – Mesomania 9
Chapter 4 – Why it Matters 11
Section A: What Causes Mesomania? 13
Chapter 5 – Early Origins 15
Chapter 6 – Joseph Smith 17
Chapter 7 – Joseph's Associates 29
Chapter 8 – The Two-Cumorahs Theory 33
Chapter 9 – What Happened to Cumorah? 35
Chapter 10 – Imprinting 41
Chapter 11 – Reinforcement 47
Chapter 12 – Enforcement 51
Section B: The Symptoms 53
Chapter 13 – You know it's Mesomania when. 55
Chapter 14 – Book of Mormon Central 57
Chapter 15 – Meridian Magazine 59
Chapter 16 – BYU Studies 60
Chapter 17 – BYU Religious Studies Center 61
Chapter 18 – Interpreter 62
Chapter 19 – FairMormon 63
Chapter 20 – More Good Foundation 64
Chapter 21 – Ancient America Foundation 65
Chapter 22 – Book of Mormon Onomasticon 66
Chapter 23 – Chiasmus Resources and Scripture Citation Index 67

Chapter 24 – BMAF 68
Chapter 25 –Maxwell Institute/ FARMS 69
Chapter 26 – LDS Scholars 71
Section C: Five Cures 73
Chapter 27 – Letter VII 75
Chapter 28 – Plains, Zelph, and Indians 77
Chapter 29 – Archaeology, Geology, etc. 78
Chapter 30 – Expectations from the text 79
Chapter 31 – Moroni's America 81
Chapter 32 – Looking Forward 83
Chapter 33 – Executive Summary 85
Appendix I: Agree/Disagree Tables 87
Appendix II: Cumorah and Book of Mormon Geography 113

Mesomania

Samuel the Lamanite
By Arnold Friberg

This painting was first published in *The Children's Friend*, a Church magazine for children, in the 1950s. For decades, it has been published in missionary editions of the Book of Mormon.

Millions of people around the world have formed first impressions of the Book of Mormon based on this depiction of massive stone walls with Mayan motifs. But the text describes nothing of the sort.

Mesomania

Classic Quotations

"we further declare that the *somewhere* of the Book of Mormon is the geographic territory known as Mesoamerica, which, in general, involves territory from Mexico City on the north to the western parts of El Salvador and Honduras on the south. **We maintain that all the actual New World events of the Book of Mormon took place within that territory.**"[1]

"There remain Latter-day Saints who insist that the final destruction of the Nephites took place in New York, but any such idea is **manifestly absurd**. Hundreds of thousands of Nephites traipsing across the Mississippi Valley to New York, pursued (why?) by hundreds of thousands of Lamanites, **is a scenario worthy only of a witless sci-fi movie, not of history.**"[2]

"Although Joseph Fielding Smith was adamant in his opinon, the data upon which the opinion was based are not nearly as strong as his statement suggests.… **The New York hill cannot be the Cumorah described in the text…** Rather than being able to use Joseph as the foundation of the naming tradition, it is easier, according to the evidence of history, to see Joseph as accepting the tradition."[3]

Opening Exercises

Exercise #1: Close your eyes a moment and visualize the Book of Mormon.

Did you picture Samuel the Lamanite standing on a high wall in a Mayan city, arrows flying toward him?

Or Christ standing in the midst of Mayan ruins?

Of course you did.

Because… Mesomania.

Despite what you've been taught, the Book of Mormon did not take place in Mesoamerica.

Why do I say that?

Because Joseph Smith and Oliver Cowdery declared that the Hill Cumorah is in New York.

Maybe you're thinking, *I already knew that.*

But most LDS scholars and educators don't believe the Hill Cumorah is in New York! They may not tell you that, but it's true. Instead, they think the Hill Cumorah is somewhere in southern Mexico.

Exercise #2: If you have a blue missionary edition of the Book of Mormon, or a foreign language version, go get it. Open it up. Look at the pictures in the front. If you don't have one, go to lds.org/scriptures, click on Book of Mormon, and then click on Illustrations.

You'll see Alma baptizing in a mountainous jungle—a Mayan wilderness. Samuel the Lamanite standing on that Mayan wall. Christ appearing to the Nephites on the steps of Mayan ruins.

Count the number of times you've seen these images. Think of all the places you've seen them.

Now, can you picture the Book of Mormon in any other location?

Exercise #3: Imagine yourself as an investigator, a kid in Primary, or a Seminary student paying attention for the first time. You've never read the Book of Mormon before. Look at the images again.

What do you expect to find when you open the book? Jungles, stone cities, pyramids, and Mayans.

Now you're you again. If you've read the Book of Mormon, you know it never once mentions jungles, or stone cities, or pyramids—let alone Mayans.

Do you see why first-time readers might be disappointed?

If we want people to read and accept the Book of Mormon, we can't keep misleading them about the setting.

It's time for Mesomania to go.

It's time to get back to what Joseph and Oliver taught us in the first place.

Huge Caveat – It's Okay to Have Different Ideas

People have lots of different beliefs about Book of Mormon geography.

They also have different *reasons* for their beliefs.

In this book, I'm focusing on the actual, real-world setting for the Book of Mormon. It's a question of historicity; i.e., the historical reality of the Book of Mormon as an authentic ancient text.

But not everyone cares about that.

Nephi told us to "liken the scriptures" unto ourselves. Some people do that by interpreting the text to describe the area where they live.

If you live in Colombia or Panama or Mexico or Ohio or New York, you might envision Zarahemla and Cumorah in your area. You might relate to the text by thinking of Lehi, Nephi, Mormon and Moroni as *your* ancestors.

That's perfectly legitimate.

We're *supposed* to apply to the teachings and messages in the text to ourselves.

In this sense, there is no right or wrong idea about Book of Mormon geography.

Mesomania

Although the dominant theory among LDS scholars and educators focuses on Mesoamerica, other people think of Chile, Peru, Colombia, Panama, Baja, and other Latin American locations. Some people think of Sri Lanka, Malaysia, or places in Africa. Settings in North America range from New York State exclusively to the entire continent.

You can even use an abstract map if you want.

Or, you can believe the Book of Mormon is a long parable—that it's not an actual history but a universal depiction of gospel principles and good vs. evil.

If these approaches work for you, great. No problem at all. Move on to chapter 32.

But consider this: one of the main purposes of the Book of Mormon is to reaffirm the authenticity of the Bible. How could it accomplish this if it is not itself an actual history of real people in a real place?

If the Book of Mormon is an authentic ancient text, obviously ancient Zarahemla and Cumorah must be in one place.

And Joseph Smith told us where it was.

We've just spent decades ignoring what he said.

Bottom line: Either you care about authenticity and accept that the Hill Cumorah is in New York, or you don't. If you don't, it doesn't really matter where you think it is, because you're not dealing with an authentic setting anyway. Which is fine, so long as you realize the implications.

Chapter 1 – The Year 2016

2016 has been an awesome year for the Book of Mormon.

Because of Church growth since 2012 (the last year the Book of Mormon was the topic of Gospel Doctrine class), more people have read and studied the Book of Mormon in 2016 than ever before in history.

Many thousands of people—Church members as well as investigators—have strengthened their testimonies as a result and gained greater appreciation for this important book of scripture.

Thousands of Church members have also come to understand and accept the North American setting for the Book of Mormon. The number increases daily.

They—we—are making Cumorah great again.

So what's this book about?
That depends on *when* you're reading it.

If you're reading in the year 2016, this book is about Book of Mormon geography.

If you're reading in 2017 or later, it is a book about history.

Why the difference?

As of September 2016 (when the book was released), some LDS scholars continue to claim the Book of Mormon took place in Central America.

Mayan themes still dominate Church media. A few months ago, a Mayan temple was constructed as a stage on the Hill Cumorah—in upstate New York.

We realize it makes no sense to construct a Mayan temple in New York, even for the Pageant. The Mayan theme is a relic of a mistake in Church history that led people to believe in a Mayan setting.

It is a symptom of Mesomania.

Thanks to Oliver Cowdery's Letter VII, rediscovered during 2016 by thousands of Church members, we understand the Hill Cumorah in New York is the very place where the Jaredite and Nephite nations fought their final battles.

Cumorah is a pin in the map that answers the question: Where did the Book of Mormon took place?

2016 has been the tipping point for Book of Mormon geography because a lot of things came to light that answered once-perplexing questions.

That's why, if you're reading in 2017 or later, you just want to know how we as a people got diverted to Mesoamerica in the first place.

Chapter 2 – It's Okay to Discuss Geography

Some people think Book of Mormon geography is a forbidden topic.

It's not.

True, the Church has no official position on the geography question. But why should it?

Book of Mormon geography is left up to the members to resolve. Finding answers is a matter of personal interest, avocation, and commitment.

Just like finding answers about every other gospel-related topic. It's called free agency.

Some Mormons think the discussion about geography is controversial, contentious, complex, confusing, or courageous.

It may be all of those (and more) for some people. But it shouldn't be.

Book of Mormon geography is actually simple and straightforward. It ought to bring people together, strengthen testimony, and increase understanding of the message of this amazing book of scripture.

And I think it will, once we recognize Mesomania and how to cure it.

Mesomania

The following two maps are all you need to know about Book of Mormon geography. Simple. Read *Moroni's America* if you want to know more.

Figure 1 - Lehi and Mulek cross the Atlantic Ocean

Figure 2 – Two pins in the map explain Book of Mormon geography

Chapter 3 – Mesomania

The transition from the Mesoamerican setting to the North American setting was long overdue.

In retrospect, it was obvious where the Book of Mormon took place. Oliver and Joseph told us, in no uncertain terms. Cumorah is in New York, the plains of the Nephites were in the Midwestern United States, and the Lamanites are the Native American Indians from the Great Lakes area.

If Book of Mormon geography is so simple, why was it not been resolved long before 2016?

The short answer: because of *Mesomania*.

At the outset, let's be clear on an important point. Faithful LDS scholars have contributed important insights into the Book of Mormon from a variety of perspectives. Some of these scholars have also promoted the Mesoamerican theory of Book of Mormon geography. As we'll see, it was not an irrational interpretation of the facts as they were once known. We respect these scholars and don't question their motives.

But we don't have to accept what they say.

The *Meso* part of Mesomania refers to Mesoamerica, a subset of Central America that is defined in cultural and historical terms and includes southern Mexico, Belize, Guatemala and El Salvador.

The *Mania* part is not a clinical reference or an illness; the term invokes the human experience of *euphoria*, *great excitement*, *excessive enthusiasm*, and, yes, *obsession*.

Mesoamerica is a tourist destination. Mesomania is a natural response to the exotic Mayan ruins—as well as the spectacular beaches and resorts.

That's not the Mesomania this book is about.

In the Mormon context, Mesomania is a distinctive way of viewing the Book of Mormon. It's a visual and mental filter, like polarized 3D glasses that block unwanted light.

Mormons who experience Mesomania read the text through Mesoamerican lenses. They not only *see* Mesoamerica in the text; they can't *unsee* it.

Most Mormons have been exposed to Mesomania, starting in Primary. Some are more susceptible than others. Some have natural resistance. Some are carriers, unaffected by the condition.

But for others, it is a very serious condition, indeed.

That's why I use the paradigm of *cause*, *symptom*, and *cure* metaphorically to frame the history and implications of Mesomania.

Chapter 4 – Why it Matters

Does it matter where the Book of Mormon took place?

That depends on you.

We each fit somewhere on the spectrum of faith vs. skepticism. It's not a spectrum of good vs. evil. People just see things differently. "And as all have not faith, seek learning… even by study and also by faith."

Just for fun, see if any of the following descriptions apply to you—or someone you know. Go ahead and check off any statements you relate to. I've known people in each of these categories.

"Geography doesn't matter" people.
Church members:
__ I have a spiritual testimony that doesn't rely on physical evidence or geography.
__ I've always believed the Book of Mormon and I don't care where it took place.
__ The purpose of the Book of Mormon is to testify of Christ, so the geography is a distraction. People either have faith or they don't and the geography isn't going to make a difference.

__ I think the Book of Mormon is a parable, not an actual history, so it doesn't matter where it took place. The teachings are the main purpose.

__ The geography question is contentious so I don't want to get involved.

Nonmembers:

__ I don't believe the Book of Mormon is true, so the geography doesn't matter anyway

---

"Geography matters" people.

Church members:

__ I have a spiritual testimony but I want confirmation from physical evidence.

__ I love the Book of Mormon and I want to understand it the way I understand the Bible better when I visit the Holy Land, and when I visit Church history sites to understand the D&C.

__ I want to believe the Book of Mormon but I need to know it is an authentic history of real people.

__ I believe the Book of Mormon but I have loved ones and friends who question its authenticity.

Nonmembers:

__ I'd be interested in the Book of Mormon if Mormons could tell me where it took place.

__ The idea that the Book of Mormon is an actual history of real people is intriguing.

Section A: What Causes Mesomania?

Mesomania is a fascination with Mesoamerica that, in the Mormon context, causes one to "see" the text through Mesoamerican lenses.

The individual

1) interprets the text as a description of Mayan society, and

2) interprets Mayan society as what is described in the text.

In this section, we'll look first at what Joseph and his associates taught about geography, then at the historical development of Mesomania and finally how Mesomania has influenced scholarly interpretation of historical events, the text of the Book of Mormon, and archaeology, anthropology, geology, and geography.

―⇢⇉ ⇇⇠―

Assumptions

First, I assume you are at least somewhat familiar with the Book of Mormon and its origins; i.e., Joseph Smith was directed by an angel to gold plates buried in a hill in New York; he translated them by the power of God and with the assistance of Oliver Cowdery; and the book is a record of the ancient inhabitants of America. There were two major groups of immigrants, the Jaredites and the Nephites, and both came to their demise in horrific battles at the Hill Cumorah.

Second, I assume you know some basics about Church history; i.e., Joseph Smith published the translation as the Book of Mormon; he organized a Church; he and his followers moved from New York to Kirtland, Ohio, then to Missouri, and then to Nauvoo, Illinois. Joseph was assassinated in 1844 and the Mormons moved to Utah.

Third, I assume you've seen the ubiquitous Mayan-themed illustrations of Book of Mormon. You've seen the hourglass-shaped maps. Maybe you've read books and articles by LDS scholars who relate passages in the text to Mayan culture and settings. Maybe you've attended the annual Pageants in New York or Manti, Utah.

Fourth, I assume you know there have been many theories of Book of Mormon geography over the years. For a hundred years, Church members and leaders agreed that Cumorah was in New York. Beyond that, some people thought the narrative extended as far as Chile. Now, in 2016, most people think the Nephites lived in a smaller area. Appendix 1 compares the two major theories, point-by-point.

Finally, I assume you already have an opinion about Book of Mormon geography. You may have strong feelings about your beliefs.

Chapter 5 – Early Origins

When Joseph Smith and Oliver Cowdery worked on the translation of the Book of Mormon in April-June of 1829, they had a simple system. Joseph dictated; Oliver wrote.

Oliver wrote the entire manuscript by hand, twice, first as Joseph spoke it, and second as a copy for the printer.

The two young men (Joseph was 24, Oliver 25) often discussed the things they were translating. They shared profound spiritual experiences, including the angelic visitations of John the Baptist and Peter, James, and John.

As one of the Three Witnesses, Oliver saw the plates and other artifacts. Later, he and Joseph visited the room in the Hill Cumorah where Mormon had stored all the records of the Nephites (Mormon 6:6).

In December 1834, Joseph set Oliver apart as Assistant President of the Church. Together, they also wrote a series of eight letters about Church history that was the first detailed account of the early events of the Restoration. Letter VII, published in July 1835, stated it was a fact that the final battles of the Jaredites and Nephites took place in the mile-wide valley west of the Hill Cumorah. This was the same hill in New York where Joseph obtained the original plates from Moroni.

Joseph had his scribes copy all eight letters into his journal as part of his own history.

A few months later, in April 1836, Joseph and Oliver, as President and Assistant President of the Church, were praying in the Kirtland temple when Moses, Elias, Elijah, and the Lord Himself appeared to them and conferred additional keys of the restoration.

How did Oliver know that the hill was the scene of these final battles?

Maybe Moroni had told Oliver or Joseph—or both of them—about what happened in that area. Maybe one or both of them had a revelation—a vision—of the ancient events that took place there. If so, they did not leave a written account of their experiences, so far as we know.

Regardless of any such revelation, Oliver would know the hill in New York was Cumorah because he and Joseph had visited Mormon's record repository.

During Joseph's lifetime, and during the lifetime of everyone who knew him, there was no uncertainty about Cumorah being in New York.

Then, in the 1920s, something changed.

We'll talk about the 1920s in Chapter 8, but first, let's take a closer look at what Joseph and his associates said they knew.

Chapter 6 – Joseph Smith

Before we discuss the 1920s, we have to address two important questions.

First, what did Joseph Smith teach about Book of Mormon archaeology?

Second, what did Joseph's contemporaries say about Book of Mormon archaeology?

To answer these questions, we need to figure out how we know what Joseph Smith *actually taught*, as opposed to what others claim or infer he taught.

We have the canonized latter-day scriptures we all accept. But beyond the scriptures, much of what is attributed to Joseph in books and lesson manuals cannot be directly attributed to him. He wrote relatively little. For example, we have no examples of the words *Mormon, Moroni, Cumorah, Bible, Aaron,* or *Melchizedek* in his own handwriting.

Like many busy people, Joseph relied on scribes and clerks to write what he dictated. Sometimes he simply directed that something be written on his behalf. Maybe he reviewed such writings, and maybe not. On June 12, 1842, Wilford Woodruff wrote a letter to Parley P. Pratt, relating that "I have never seen Joseph as full of business as of late **he hardly gets time to sign his name**"[4] (emphasis added).

In most cases, there is no evidence that Joseph dictated or reviewed documents he did not personally sign. Instead, we look at circumstances and content to assess whether they should be attributed to Joseph.

This chapter is a brief overview of some of the most significant documents relating to Book of Mormon geography created during Joseph Smith's lifetime. If you don't want to read about each of these documents, here is the executive summary:

1. Neither Joseph nor any of his associates ever questioned the New York setting for the Hill Cumorah.

2. Everything that can be directly attributed to Joseph Smith puts the Book of Mormon in North America, specifically within the territory of the United States circa 1842.

3. Not a single document that connects the Book of Mormon with Central or South America can be directly linked to Joseph Smith.

During Zion's Camp in 1834, Joseph led a group of Saints from Ohio to Missouri. While stopped in Illinois on the banks of the Mississippi River on June 4, waiting to cross, Joseph wrote a letter to Emma. We don't have the original letter, but we have the original Letterbook that Joseph's scribes used to record copies of his correspondence. Because it is unlikely that Joseph would ask someone else to write to Emma, and because we have other letters Joseph wrote to Emma, we have high confidence that this letter was originally written by Joseph to his wife.

The camp had crossed most of Ohio, Indiana and Illinois. Joseph described it to Emma this way:

> The whole of our journey, in the midst of so large a company of social honest and sincere men, **wandering over the plains of the Nephites**, recounting occasionally the history of the Book of Mormon, **roving over the mounds of that once beloved people of the Lord, picking up their skulls and their bones, as a proof of its divine authenticity**... (emphasis added)

In the Book of Mormon, both the Nephites and the Jaredites mention plains (See Appendix 1).

A day earlier, on June 3, 1844, Joseph and other members of Zion's Camp ascended a large mound not far from the Illinois River, about 100 miles southeast of Nauvoo. They uncovered a large skeleton that had an atlatl head—a large arrowhead—stuck in the bones. Several of the brethren recorded in their journals that Joseph had a vision about the individual, whose name was Zelph. Wilford Woodruff recorded that Joseph explained

Mesomania

> Zelph was a large thick set man and a man of God. He was a warrior under the great prophet /Onandagus/ that was known from **the hill Camorah /or east sea/** to the Rocky mountains.

See Appendix 1 for more detail.

Although their accounts vary slightly, multiple witnesses make this a reliable account.

The letter to Emma and the Zelph vision are two reliable, credible teachings of Joseph Smith that place the Book of Mormon firmly in the Midwestern region of the United States.

Mesomania lens. When viewed through the Mesomania lens, these incidents are explained as taking place in the "Hinterlands," meaning Book of Mormon people who migrated north, outside the territory of the narrative. The specific phrase "plains of the Nephites" is never used in the Book of Mormon, so Joseph was not referring to Book of Mormon sites. He was merely speculating about the mounds being Nephite in origin. And Zelph, who was never mentioned in the text, was involved with some other wars, probably postdating Book of Mormon times.

About a year later, in July 1935 [1839], Oliver published Letter VII, one of the series of eight letters about Church history I mentioned in the previous chapter. Oliver wrote these with the assistance of Joseph Smith.

Mesomania

Letter VII appeared in the July 1835 *Messenger and Advocate*, the Church newspaper in Kirtland, Ohio.

In October 1835, Joseph directed his scribes to copy all of the letters into his journal as part of "a history of my life."

Joseph later gave Benjamin Winchester permission to reprint the letters in Winchester's Philadelphia newspaper called the *Gospel Reflector*. It appeared in the March 1841 edition.

Joseph's brother Don Carlos, editor and publisher of the *Times and Seasons* in Nauvoo, reprinted Letter VII in the April 1841 edition.

During Joseph's lifetime, no one questioned the New York location of Cumorah. Not a single one of his associates did, either.

Mesomania lens. When viewed through the Mesomania lens, Letter VII is merely Oliver's speculation. Worse, Oliver was wrong, and Joseph passively adopted Oliver's mistake as his own.

A thank-you note written in Joseph's name to Dr. Bernhisel, a Church member in New York City, is dated November 16, 1841.

Although it is written in the first person and signed "Joseph Smith," no one knows who actually wrote the letter because the handwriting has never been identified. It is neither Joseph's, nor that of any of the clerks and scribes that took his dictation.

Most likely, the letter was drafted by Wilford Woodruff and written out by someone with good penmanship.[5] Unless and until we identify the handwriting, we cannot be sure about any of this.

The thank-you note expresses great interest in a two-volume set of books about Central America written by John Lloyd Stephens. Dr. Bernhisel gave the books to Woodruff to give to Joseph Smith.

> **Mesomania lens.** Even though we know Joseph didn't write the letter, the note proves Joseph enthusiastically embraced Central America as the setting for the Book of Mormon.

Some of the most widely known teachings about geography that have been attributed to Joseph Smith are found in the printed pages of the 1842 *Times and Seasons* (the Church newspaper in Nauvoo).

There are three categories of material in the 1842 *Times and Seasons*:

1) Signed by the author (or citing a source)
2) Anonymous
3) Pseudonymous

1) Articles signed by Joseph Smith as the author, or directly claimed by Joseph Smith, include the Book of Abraham, D&C 127 and 128, the Wentworth letter (which includes the Articles of Faith). However, we

only have the printed versions; we have no original handwritten manuscripts.

We do have the original manuscripts of Joseph Smith-History (now in the Pearl of Great Price), but they were written by clerks, not by Joseph himself. This history does not name Cumorah; verse 51 refers merely to a "hill of considerable size, and the most elevated of any in the neighborhood."

> **Mesomania lens.** The failure of Joseph's clerks to use the term Cumorah indicates that the hill is not, in fact, the Book of Mormon Cumorah.

The Wentworth letter is a brief history of the Church, signed in print by Joseph Smith. The Wentworth letter is largely taken from an 1840 pamphlet written by Orson Pratt that claimed Book of Mormon people lived throughout Latin America. However, Joseph edited out that entire section to clarify that the remnant of Lehi's people are "the Indians that now inhabit this country." Joseph wrote from Nauvoo, Illinois, to Mr. Wentworth in Chicago, Illinois; i.e., they lived in the same *country*, whether you interpret that to mean *nation* or *area*. This statement about the Indians is consistent with D&C 28, 30 and 32, which identify these tribes as Lamanites, and directly contradicts the Mesoamerican setting.

> **Mesomania lens.** The Mesomania lens interprets "this country" to mean "the entire Western

Mesomania

hemisphere." "Indians" refers to all the indigenous tribes, including the Mayans. D&C 28, 30, and 32 reflect an early understanding that these tribes were Lamanites, but that was mere speculation and it was incorrect.

D&C 128:20 refers to Cumorah along with other sites in New York and Pennsylvania.

Mesomania lens. Verse 20 is actually referring to the real Hill Cumorah somewhere in Mexico, or is paying homage to that hill.

2) Three anonymous articles in the September 15 and October 1 issues of the *Times and Seasons* contain long extracts from the Stephens books. The anonymous editorial comments claim that Zarahemla was in Quirigua, Guatemala, and that Lehi "landed a little south of the Isthmus of Darien." The ruins referenced in the extracts post-date Book of Mormon time frames. For a variety of reasons, Joseph could not have written these articles; instead, they were written by Benjamin Winchester and edited by William Smith and/or W.W. Phelps.[6]

Mesomania lens. One lens insists Joseph wrote these anonymous articles, possibly with the assistance of Wilford Woodruff and/or John Taylor. Another lens agrees Joseph did not write the articles but claims it doesn't matter because Mesomania doesn't rely on these articles in the first place.

These articles have been frequently cited to support Mesomania. As shown in the introductory pages of this book, the articles were featured at the 2005 Library of Congress symposium on Joseph Smith—one of the highest profile efforts to tell the world about the Prophet.

Because some scholars continue to argue that they show Joseph Smith embraced the Central American setting, or at least that he was open to it, I'll take a moment to look at the rationale for attributing these articles to Joseph Smith.

From February 15 through October 15, 1842, Joseph Smith was listed at the end of the *Times and Seasons* as editor, printer, and publisher. Ever since, people have assumed this meant Joseph wrote, or at least approved of, every *unattributed* article in the paper. This is based on an overly literal interpretation of the boilerplate[7] inserted at the end of every issue.[8]

The boilerplate said the paper was "edited, printed and published" by Joseph Smith. Surely no one believes Joseph literally *printed* the paper; that would require him to spend his time at the print shop, setting type and operating the printing press.

There is no more reason to conclude that Joseph literally *edited* the paper.

Furthermore, there is no actual evidence that Joseph Smith edited the newspaper. Instead, the evidence indicates he was merely the *nominal* editor—

the named editor. He delegated the editing duties to others, just like he did with the printing duties.

That's the simple explanation.

It means Joseph had nothing to do with the Central American articles. If you're satisfied with that answer, go to Chapter 7. For the rest of you, we're going to look at more historical detail.

Here is the boilerplate in the *Times and Seasons*:

Figure 2 - T&S boilerplate Feb 15-June 15, 1842

The Times and Seasons,
IS EDITED BY
Joseph Smith.
Printed and published about the first and fifteenth of every month, on the corner of Water and Bain Streets, Nauvoo, Hancock County, Illinois, by
JOSEPH SMITH.
TERMS.—Two Dollars per annum, payable in all cases in advance. Any person procuring five new subscribers, and forwarding us Ten Dollars current money, shall receive one volume gratis. All letters must be addressed to Joseph Smith, publisher, post paid, or they will not receive attention.

If it looks odd to repeat his name this way, they did it to save money. In the previous issue, the duties were divided between two people.

When Joseph took over, they just replaced those names with his to save time and money.

Figure 3 - T&S boilerplate February 1, 1842

> **The Times and Seasons,**
> IS EDITED BY
> E. ROBINSON, & G. HILLS.
> Printed and published about the first and fifteenth of every month, on the corner of Water and Bain Streets, Nauvoo, Hancock County, Illinois, by
> E. ROBINSON.
> TERMS.—Two DOLLARS per annum, payable in all cases in advance. Any person procuring five new subscribers, and forwarding us Ten Dollars current money, shall receive one volume gratis. All letters must be addressed to E. Robinson, publisher, POST PAID, or they will not receive attention.

Later, to avoid the awkward repetition of Joseph's name, the boilerplate was changed beginning with the July 1, 1842, issue of the *Times and Seasons*.

Figure 4 - T&S boilerplate Jul 1 - Oct 15, 1842

> **The Times and Seasons,**
> Is edited, printed and published about the first and fifteenth of every month, on the corner of Water and Bain Streets, Nauvoo, Hancock County, Illinois, by
> JOSEPH SMITH
> TERMS.—Two DOLLARS per annum, payable in all cases in advance. Any person procuring five new subscribers, and forwarding us Ten Dollars current money, shall receive one volume gratis. All letters must be addressed to Joseph Smith, publisher, POST PAID, or they will not receive attention.

Mesomania

The boilerplate should not be interpreted to mean Joseph literally edited, printed, and published every edition.

The *Times and Seasons* was not even the first newspaper to list Joseph Smith as Editor of a paper he didn't actually edit. The *Elders' Journal*, a newspaper published in Kirtland, Ohio, in 1837, showed Joseph as Editor even though his brother Don Carlos was the actual editor. (Don Carlos later became the original editor of the *Times and Seasons* in Nauvoo.)

That's about it as far as Joseph Smith's teachings about Book of Mormon geography. On a few occasions, he met with Indian tribes to tell them their fathers wrote the Book of Mormon. That corroborates the North American setting but is still a little vague.

To summarize, **there is not a single document that can be directly linked to Joseph Smith that says anything about the Book of Mormon and Central America. Every document that can be directly linked to Joseph describes a North American setting.**

Chapter 7 – Joseph's Associates

Many scholars assume that Joseph Smith's associates knew what he believed about topics he didn't otherwise discuss publicly. That assumption in turn relies on the assumption that Joseph told what he knew to his close associates.

Cascading assumptions are tenuous enough, but in this case, they contradict the evidence and common human experience. How many of us tell our associates *everything* we think about *every* topic? Even if we wanted to, it's not even possible.

On November 1, 1844, just months after the martyrdom, Woodruff recorded this in his journal:

> I also had another dream. Was in the Presence of Br Joseph Smith. Was conversing about his death. Told him I felt bad about it & **If I had known he would have been taken away so soon I should have conversed more with him & asked him more questions. Said it was not his fault that I did not.**

The assumption Joseph's closest associates knew what he thought about every topic is more wishful thinking than a historically verified, or even feasible, reality.

True, there were instances when reliable people recorded what Joseph actually said, but even then the accounts are not identical. Examples are the King Follet sermon and the Zelph mound incident.

There have been instances when people related, long after the fact, what they remembered. The reliability and credibility of these witnesses, the plausibility of the statements, and any corroborating evidence must be assessed on a case-by-case basis.

With this in mind, we can evaluate the various statements about Book of Mormon geography by W.W. Phelps, William Smith, Orson Pratt, Benjamin Winchester, Wilford Woodruff, John E. Page, and others.[9] These statements have been compiled and analyzed by many others. There is considerable variety, suggesting these men were speculating about the geography question.

In the early days of the Church, Mormon authors fought against anti-Mormon factions. One of the big issues then (as it is today) was the authenticity of the Book of Mormon.

Some critics said Joseph Smith copied the book from other authors who had written about the American Indians. Others said the Indians were too primitive to have the complex society described in the Book of Mormon.

In response, early Mormon authors pointed to evidence of ancient civilizations on the American continent. There were massive, complex earth mounds in North America and stunning stone pyramids and cities in Central America.

The Mayan ruins, of course, were more impressive. They attracted the attention of the public, particularly in 1841 when John Lloyd Stephens published his bestselling books that contained Catherwood's famous drawings of the ruins. (These are the books extracted in the anonymous *Times and Seasons* articles.)

Joseph's associates figured that linking the Book of Mormon to these remarkable sites would attract public attention to the book. People would transfer their Stephens-inspired Mesomania to the Book of Mormon, read the book, and be converted.

These early authors had the first cases of *Mormon* Mesomania. And they didn't realize it.

They also didn't seem to realize that when people are promised a book about ancient Mayan civilization, they are inevitably disappointed to discover the book never mentions pyramids, jungles, jaguars or tapirs.

Or even Mayans, for that matter.

In retrospect, it seems obvious why the American public didn't buy the connection between the Book of Mormon and Central America. Stephens himself estimated that the ruins dated to several hundred years after the Book of Mormon time frames.

Yet Mormon authors continued to try to make the connection.

Mesomania

None of the early Mormon authors claimed Joseph Smith told them the Book of Mormon took place anywhere outside of what was then the United States.

We have Joseph and Oliver specifically identifying the Hill Cumorah in New York. We have Joseph identifying the plains of the Nephites in the Ohio, Indiana, and Illinois. We have Joseph's vision of Zelph in Illinois. We have the specific D&C references to the Lamanites in the United States.

But we don't have a single reference to Central or South America that can be directly attributed to Joseph Smith.

We can understand why the early Mormon authors, in their enthusiastic zeal to spread the gospel, would latch onto a popular obsession with Mesoamerica. The public as a whole caught Mesomania in the 1840s, so why not ride the wave?

The public didn't respond as hoped. People recognized the Book of Mormon describes anything *but* Mesoamerica. Mormon Mesomania didn't catch on.

Except among a handful of RLDS scholars, who then transmitted it to a handful of LDS scholars.

All they needed was an explanation for Cumorah.
And they invented one.
It's called the two-Cumorahs theory.

Chapter 8 – The Two-Cumorahs Theory

Beginning in the 1920s, scholars from the Reorganized Church of Jesus Christ of Latter-day Saints adopted a "limited geography" theory that placed Book of Mormon events in Central America (Mesoamerica). They calculated that the entire Book of Mormon took place within about an 800-mile radius of locations in Central America.[10]

The hill in New York—3,000 miles from Guatemala—was considered too far away to be the Book of Mormon Cumorah.

That's a reasonable conclusion, actually, once you accept the Mesoamerican theory.

But the limited geography created an apparent dilemma—the New York Cumorah can't co-exist with a Guatemalan Zarahemla.

Book of Mormon scholars had to choose between the two settings.

How would you resolve this conflict?

The scholars decided that the hill in New York was *misnamed* Cumorah. They figured early Church members applied the name because Joseph obtained the plates there. It was a tradition, and Joseph Smith just went along with it.

The "real" Cumorah—the scene of the final battles of the Jaredites and the Nephites—had to be somewhere in Central America, along with Zarahemla and the other Book of Mormon sites. Perhaps the anonymous 1842 *Times and Seasons* articles influenced this choice; i.e., the articles implied that Joseph Smith agreed with the Central American setting.

Having made their decision, LDS scholars have spent decades looking for evidence of the Book of Mormon in Central America.

By the 1980s, the limited geography Mesoamerican theory appeared in the *Ensign* magazine. It became the consensus among LDS scholars and educators who focused on the Book of Mormon. Over the years, they have written dozens of papers and books about similarities, or "correspondences," between Mayan civilization and what they read in the text, a process they call finding Mesoamerica in the text.

In 2016, the well-funded Book of Mormon Central organization began promoting Mesomania in daily outreach messages.

But whatever happened to Cumorah?

Chapter 9 – What Happened to Cumorah?

Pretend you're a Book of Mormon scholar for a moment. You believe in the Mesoamerican setting. How do you handle Cumorah?

It's easy to reject the New York Cumorah because, at 3,000 miles from your Central American Zarahemla, it's just too far. You just say it doesn't fit your theory. Forget about New York, you say.

But you have members of the Church who accept Letter VII and the other statements of Joseph Smith. And you have Joseph Fielding Smith's unmistakable affirmation that Cumorah is in New York.

Easy, you respond. Oliver and Joseph were speculating. They misread Mormon 6:6. They never claimed revelation, so their guess is as good as anyone's. As for Joseph Fielding Smith, he didn't know much about the facts. He, too, was speculating.

The question can only be resolved by scholarship, unless and until modern prophets claim revelation on a par with the Book of Mormon itself.

Your arguments take hold, especially in the academic community, which trains the educators. Soon most people agree with you; Cumorah is not in

New York. You end up with the Classic Quotations at the beginning of this book.

> **Mesomania lens:** One BYU scholar explained the scholarly consensus about the location of the Book of Mormon in Central America: "Actually, the Limited Geography Model does not insist that there were two Cumorahs. Rather, there was one Cumorah in Mesoamerica, which is always the hill referred to in the Book of Mormon. Thereafter, beginning with Oliver Cowdery (possibly based on a misreading of Mormon 6:6), early Mormons began to associate the Book of Mormon Cumorah with the hill in New York where Joseph Smith found the plates. The Book of Mormon itself is internally consistent on the issue. It seems to have been early nineteenth-century Latter-day Saint interpretation of the text of the Book of Mormon which has caused the confusion on this point. Thus, advocates of the Limited Geography Model are required only to show that their interpretations are consistent with the text of the Book of Mormon itself, not with any nineteenth-century interpretation of the Book of Mormon."[11]

🖋 But still, there are holdouts. The argument that Letter VII is a misreading of Mormon 6:6 by Joseph and Oliver seems dubious to members of the Church. People wonder, how could modern scholars understand the Book of Mormon better than the two men who translated it, who handled the plates, who met Moroni, who visited the Nephite records repository, and who asked the Lord when they encountered passages that raised questions?

Some of the holdout members have read the book by Willard Bean and Cecil McGavin. Willard and his wife were called by Joseph F. Smith in 1915 to move to Palmyra. They were the first LDS to live in the town in 84 years. They stayed there for 25 years and were instrumental in purchasing the Hill Cumorah and other important sites.

Bean and McGavin wrote a book titled *Book of Mormon Geography: In Search of Ramah-Cumorah*. They documented numerous ancient fortifications in the area that corroborate Letter VII.

So as a scholar, how do you respond?

You put on your Mesomania lens to look at the question of geography.

> **Mesomania lens:** Maybe in 1981 you write a book titled *In Search of Cumorah: New Evidences for the Book of Mormon from Ancient Mexico*. In it, you attribute the anonymous *Times and Seasons* articles to Joseph Smith, dismiss Letter VII without even quoting it, and set up a list of criteria—including proximity to volcanoes—that can be satisfied only by a hill in Mexico.[12]

Or maybe you write an article in 2004 for the *Journal of Book of Mormon Studies* titled "Archaeology and Cumorah Questions." The article will become popular among Mesoamerican advocates. In it, you write,

> "… sufficient information is available for the surrounding regions to make a critical assessment. Mormon's hill and Moroni's hill are not one and the same… Archaeologically speaking, it is a clean hill. No artifacts, no walls, no trenches, no arrowheads. The area immediately surrounding the hill is similarly clean. Pre-Columbian people did not settle or build here. This is not the place of Mormon's last stand. We must look elsewhere for that hill."

You cite a PhD dissertation about a highway construction archaeological survey, claiming it provides 100 percent coverage. But you don't tell readers that the author of that dissertation said he had done only "minimal test excavations" and he lamented later that "a major proportion of the archaeological sites" identified by his research "had been destroyed without the benefit of any research beyond the work noted in this study."

You also ignore the author's observation that "Practically every landowner who has any close connection with his or her property (farming, etc.) has a collection ranging from a few stray projectile points to thousands of artifacts."[13]

Maybe you also write an article about a student's analysis of the Hill Cumorah archaeology. The student asked farmers on the east and north sides of the hill if they have ever found artifacts. They say they haven't. Therefore, you conclude, the hill is "clean" and cannot be Cumorah.

What you forgot is that Oliver Cowdery said all the battles took place on the west side of the hill, from which farmers have plowed up thousands of artifacts over the years.

Maybe best of all, you participate in the Worlds of Joseph Smith, a Bicentennial conference at the Library of Congress. *BYU Studies* publishes it as a special edition, Vol. 44, No. 4, 2005.

You put on display a page from John Lloyd Stephens' *Incidents of Travel in Central America, Chiapas, and Yucatan*, along with the cover page from the *Times and Seasons*, October 1, 1842, that features the "Zarahemla" article.

Then you tell the world that "Joseph Smith did not fully understand the Book of Mormon… Joseph speculated that Book of Mormon lands were located in Central America."

Let's review.

Mesomania

As a Book of Mormon scholar who believes in the Mesoamerican setting, you've done an excellent job.

You've discarded Letter VII by claiming Oliver misread the Book of Mormon, he was merely speculating—and he was wrong.

You've also undermined the credibility of David Whitmer, another of the Three Witnesses.

You've faulted Luck Mack Smith, Joseph's mother, for misremembering things when she wrote his history.

You've persuaded people that Joseph and Oliver never entered Mormon's repository of records in New York, but instead had a vision of a mountain somewhere in southern Mexico.

You've downplayed what Joseph actually taught, and emphasized things he didn't teach.

You've dismissed the archaeological evidence in New York and set up a series of criteria designed to fit Mesoamerica exclusively.

The question is, why have you done all of this?

Chapter 10 – Imprinting

"First impressions are lasting impressions."

Young animals learn behavioral patterns from their parents—the first beings they see. Ducklings follow their mother. Kittens bond with their mothers, and so forth. It's called imprinting.

Imprinting is essential for the survival of young animals. If they don't imitate and stay close to their parents, they are vulnerable to predators.

People also imprint. Mothers and babies form close bonds that usually last a lifetime.

Language is imprinted. You probably learned your first language from your parents. If the first language you learned was Chinese, then English is likely difficult for you. If your first language was German, you won't learn Hindi without great effort.

When people learn another language beyond a certain age, they find it nearly impossible to eliminate their accent. They can't retrain their mouth, throat, tongue, etc. Imprinting is too powerful.

The technical definition of imprinting is "any kind of phase-sensitive learning (learning occurring at a particular life stage) that is rapid and independent of the consequences of behavior."

However, a form of imprinting occurs throughout our lives. Hence the phrases, "first impressions are lasting impressions" and "you never get a second chance to make a first impression."

Brain researchers have identified the parts of the brain that register first impressions. When we have a new experience that contradicts a first impression, we tend to treat it as an exception. We constrain the new experience to its specific context, leaving the first impression to dominate in other contexts.

If you don't like your boss the first time you meet him/her, it takes a while before that first impression can change. If the first smart phone you had was an iPhone, you may find an Android phone weird.

I teach a course in film studies to mostly American students. At one point during class, I show clips of the film *Paradise Now*, a movie made by a Palestinian director about two Palestinian men preparing for a suicide attack in Israel. The students have a difficult time with the idea of humanizing suicide bombers.

Cultural influences, like first impressions, are difficult to recognize, let alone isolate and evaluate.

What does all this have to do with the Book of Mormon?

If you're a Mormon living today, you've seen the series of paintings by Arnold Friberg.

Mesomania

Notice the huge stone pyramid
Notice the temple on top.
Notice the stairs going up the center in front.
Notice the layers in the pyramid.

Mesomania

Now, look at the logos of some of the most prominent LDS scholarly organizations that focus on the Book of Mormon.

They share the same characteristics of the Friberg painting.

Notice the huge stone pyramid
Notice the temple on top.
Notice the stairs going up the center in front.
Notice the layers in the pyramid.
I don't think this is coincidental.

Mesomania

In fact, it *couldn't* be coincidental. These organizations think these logos somehow represent the Book of Mormon, but nowhere does the Book of Mormon mention pyramids, let alone pyramids with temples on top.

The Book of Mormon never even says the people constructed buildings with stone!

Instead, they built with wood and earth. In one instance, they built a wall out of stone. In one chapter, Helaman 3, a few people built out of cement, but they built with *wood* and cement, not stone and cement.

(You can see examples of wood and cement construction in North America, recreated by non-LDS archaeologists, across the river from St. Louis.)

So why would these LDS scholars choose a Mayan pyramid as a symbol of the Book of Mormon?

Because the Friberg painting imprinted the image on their minds at a young age. They probably don't even realize it.

An article in the Deseret News noted that "Friberg's classic collection of Book of Mormon paintings have captivated and stirred the imaginations of countless people for more than half a century."[14]

The paintings have been included in millions of copies of the Book of Mormon and in countless LDS media outlets. The originals are on display in the Conference Center in Salt Lake City.

Mesomania

Friberg was the chief artist-designer of the movie "The Ten Commandments" in the 1950s. The general president of the Primary wanted something special for the Primary's 50th year, so she personally paid Friberg $1,000 each to create 12 paintings to publish once a month in *The Children's Friend*.

Friberg was free to interpret the Book of Mormon however he wanted, and he understandably decided to paint dramatic scenes set in Central America. He is quoted in the article above: "It was a startling task to undertake, for the Book of Mormon had never been illustrated before, at least on any professional level."

Friberg's paintings create first impressions every time a person picks up a missionary edition of the Book of Mormon for the first time, every time a Primary child learns a lesson about Samuel the Lamanite, and every time a parent teaches a son or daughter about Abinadi.

What about you?

If possible, think back to the first time you read the Book of Mormon. See if you can envision Nephi crossing the ocean, the brother of Jared seeing the finger of the Lord, the Title of Liberty, or Ammon defending the flocks without thinking of the Friberg paintings.

Imprinting stays with us our entire lives.

Chapter 11 – Reinforcement

We wouldn't be discussing Mesomania if the Arnold Friberg paintings had appeared once in the *Children's Friend* and then dropped out of sight.

Or if they were balanced by other perspectives.

As I mentioned, these paintings have been reproduced millions of times. Plus, they have inspired other artists, including painters, authors, sculptors, film directors, and others. John Scott's painting "Jesus Teaching in the Western Hemisphere (Jesus Christ Visits the Americas)," also featured in the missionary editions of the Book of Mormon, may be even more ubiquitous than the Friberg paintings.

As influential as the arts can be, it is the incorporation of Mesoamerican art into Church curriculum and media that has reinforced the original imprint on the minds of the Latter-day Saints.

Church magazines—the *Friend* (successor to the *Children's Friend*), the New Era, the Ensign, and the Liahona—commonly use the Friberg and Scott paintings to depict Book of Mormon events. They are staples in seminary and Institute classes.

Surely more people have seen these images than have read the text itself. Even avid readers of the text have no doubt seen the artwork more frequently than they've read the verses.

This reinforcement of the Mesoamerican setting is extremely powerful.

I've spoken to scholars who are convinced that the Book of Mormon took place in mountainous terrain. When I point out that mountains are not even mentioned in the New World until Helaman 10:9, they don't believe me—until they recheck the text.

Why do they infer a mountainous terrain?

Look at *Alma Baptizing in the Waters of Mormon*.

This is a dramatic image, no doubt. But Alma hid from the king in a "thicket of small trees." No jungle or mountains are mentioned. Not even a waterfall.

Mesomania

When we reflect on this, we recognize that these paintings are just one artist's conception. They're not the gospel truth. They're not doctrine. They're not the text. But that's our conscious, rational brain speaking.

On the more subtle, subconscious, even emotional level, these paintings have been imprinted on our minds and hearts, and reinforced in untold lessons and displays. They're all derivative of Friberg.

Do you see the pyramid? It is right above the woman holding the baby. This painting, *Christ visiting the Americas* by John Scott, suggests a generic concept; i.e., it may reflect Christ visiting people not mentioned in the text. But on lds.org it is labeled *Christ teaching Nephites*. (Go to lds.org and search media for "Christ teaching nephites." You'll get the Scott painting along with one by Gary L. Kapp that shows the inevitable combination of a massive Mayan pyramid, tall mountains, and palm trees in the background.)

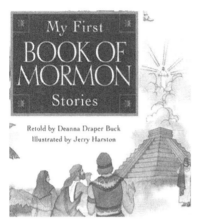

This example of a children's book has Christ appearing above the Mayan temple, clearly evoking Friberg's interpretation.

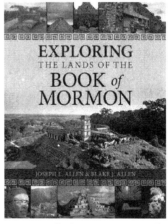

Here, a more scholarly book intended for older people continues the reinforcement through later years. (The temple is in the upper left, second image from the left margin.)

These observations are not intended as criticism of the artists and authors involved. I offer this artwork as an example of how pervasive Mesomania is.

Look around and you'll find plenty more examples. The initial imprinting we have all experienced is being reinforced constantly.

Chapter 12 – Enforcement

We've reviewed the origins of Mesomania. Joseph Smith and Oliver Cowdery unambiguously identified Cumorah in New York, and this knowledge was republished often enough that everyone during Joseph's lifetime accepted that site.

Beyond Cumorah, though, people speculated. Partly in response to anti-Mormon attacks, early Mormon authors pointed to ruins in North and Central America. When the Stephens books were published and became bestsellers, Mesomania intensified. The anonymous articles in the 1842 *Times and Seasons* were peak Mesomania. Interest in the subject yielded to survival as the Saints left for Utah.

In the 1920s, RLDS scholars developed the limited geography theory, focusing on Mesoamerica. They disregarded the New York site for Cumorah because it was too far away. Over the objection of Joseph Fielding Smith, LDS scholars agreed with the RLDS scholars and developed the Mesoamerican theory in more detail.

Arnold Friberg's paintings from the 1950s cemented Mesomania in Church culture. The paintings inspired other artists and imprinted Mesomania on the minds of every Church member born since then. They influenced the scholars who trained the educators who teach each new generation.

Through the artwork, Mesomania is reinforced on a frequent basis for Mormons who attend church and visit the temple. Every missionary uses the blue Mesoamerican editions with investigators.

On a deeper level, Mesomania is reinforced by the scholarly community through a variety of publications, presentations, conferences, and online participation.

But as we'll see, these sources not only reinforce Mesomania—they *enforce* Mesomania.

Ideally, an academic environment is a place for open discussion of a variety of perspectives on any given topic. You might think, for example, that at a BYU campus, students are encouraged to discuss Book of Mormon geography and evaluate the various alternatives.

Hardly.

You've got two 2-credit classes—Religion 121 and 122—that cover the entire Book of Mormon. Students use an abstract map to follow the geography that is shaped like an hourglass and doesn't show Cumorah.

That's it.

Anyone who wants to explore the geography and historicity must go elsewhere—meaning, the Internet.

Section B: The Symptoms

A fish doesn't know it's wet because it has always been surrounded by water. Take it out of water and it learns fast, though.

Okay, I realize that's a terrible metaphor for Mesomania. No one will die over this issue.

On the other hand, consider what Joseph Fielding Smith said. "Because of this theory some members of the Church have become confused and greatly disturbed in their faith in the Book of Mormon."

If President Smith was right, maybe in a spiritual sense the fish metaphor applies after all.

Let's revisit the caveat: "It's okay to have different ideas."

Maybe we can apply the fish metaphor by observing that some fish swim in deep water, some in shallow. Some swim in warm water, some in cold. Some swim in salt water, some in fresh. It doesn't matter so long as they're in the water (but even then, flying fish do fine—temporarily—in the air).

Let's say the metaphor for the Book of Mormon is the water. As long as we're immersed in it, we're alive (spiritually, in this metaphor).

Just because we like salt water doesn't mean a fish who likes fresh water is wrong. Different species of fish are… different.

People may be attracted to the Book of Mormon for a variety of reasons, and if one of them is because they believe the events took place where they lived, or in a culture they've studied extensively, hopefully no one will criticize them for that.

But realistically, the number of people who are immersed in the Book of Mormon is quite small.

The question is, how do we get more people in the water?

I don't think it's by confusing them.

Set aside the fish metaphor.

Now imagine you're swimming in a cool fresh lake in the middle of a desert on a hot day.

There are millions of people standing on the sand. They refuse to join you. They say the lake is a mirage.

You step out to hold their hand, to help them into the water. But when you turn around, you see what everyone else saw.

It *was* a mirage.

But in the distance, you see a clear blue lake with people splashing, and you realize that's the one you thought you were in.

Chapter 13 – You know it's Mesomania when...

The saying goes, "there is no growth in the comfort zone and no comfort in the growth zone."

The lake metaphor suggests that sometimes we have to step out of our comfort zone to see clearly.

As we've seen, most members of the Church—and most nonmembers—have been exposed to Mesomania.

For most members, it's the default position.

The comfort zone.

They might stay there forever.

But some—I think most—will eventually step out and look back. In the words of Joseph Fielding Smith, they'll become confused and greatly disturbed in their faith. Then it's a question of whether they will go along with the crowd and leave the water entirely, or whether they will notice that other lake—the one with real water in it.

Let's see if we can recognize some of the symptoms of Mesomania.

Mesomania

A lot of the material in this book is serious, so let's have a little fun.

You know it's Mesomania when…

- you haven't read Letter VII
- you haven't even *heard* of Letter VII
- you think King Noah had pet leopards
- you think Alma's "thicket of small trees" is a jungle
- you think a tapir is a horse
- you think *pyramid* when you read *tower*
- you think the Nephites engraved their history on stone everywhere
- you think Joseph Smith wrote anonymous articles for the *Times and Seasons*
- you think it is "manifestly absurd" that Cumorah is in New York
- you think Lehi crossed the Pacific Ocean
- you think you can build a map of the Book of Mormon using google Earth and the text
- you convene a group of like-minded scholars to determine the meaning of scriptural passages
- you can't unsee Mesoamerica in the Book of Mormon
- you think the Nephites sacrificed rodents under the law of Moses
- you defer to the Mesoamerican consensus because you can't picture any other setting

Chapter 14 – Book of Mormon Central

Book of Mormon Central (BOMC) is a well-funded web page that seeks to compile Book of Mormon research published by a variety of sources into one place. BOMC offers several important research aids, including Royal Skousen's analysis of the earliest manuscripts of the Book of Mormon and his version of the text based on those early manuscripts.

As of September 2016, its archive contains over 2,000 items. Most of these are from its affiliates: BMAF, the *Interpreter*, etc., as well as the Maxwell Institute. We'll look at each of these in upcoming chapters.

To its credit, BOMC has an official position of neutrality. It has published some additional material, including the first edition of my book, *Letter VII: Oliver Cowdery's Message to the World about the Hill Cumorah*. Letter VII has been the most popular item in the BOMC archive for several months.

However, BOMC is really a front for the nonprofit organization titled Ancient America Foundation (AAF). AAF has focused on Mesoamerica for decades, and this is reflected in the materials BOMC creates and disseminates.

BOMC publishes a daily (weekday) feature called a KnoWhy that analyzes a particular element of the Book of Mormon. These KnoWhys promote Mesomania whenever possible.[15]

BOMC redistributes old Mesoamerican articles and generates new Mesoamerican material. Its affiliates continue to actively promote the Mesoamerican theory.

In fact, BOMC is doubling down on Mesomania, and using a tremendous amount of resources to promote the Mesoamerican message through social media.

For these reasons, I urge caution is accessing BOMC. There are some helpful resources, but also a fixation on Mesoamerica that is regrettable.

In my opinion, BOMC is doing more harm than good for Book of Mormon studies.

That said, BOMC has the potential and infrastructure to change course and help make Cumorah great again.

Whether it will do so remains an open question.

Next, we'll look at BOMC affiliates.

Chapter 15 – Meridian Magazine

Meridian Magazine is the first affiliate listed on the Book of Mormon Central web page.[16]

The BOMC description reads, "Looking at the events of our tumultuous time through a Latter-day Saint lens, investigating pertinent and important stories, bringing you topics a reader could find nowhere else from a perspective you appreciate."

The lens part should be modified a bit, at least with regard to the Book of Mormon, because *Meridian* views the world through the Mesomania lens.

The magazine reprints every BOMC KnoWhy. The editors, Maureen and Scot Proctor, and several of the contributors are adamant about the Mesoamerican setting.

Meridian offers a wide variety of useful and entertaining content for LDS readers. As long as you realize what lenses the contributors are wearing, I recommend the magazine for non-geography topics.

Chapter 16 – BYU Studies

BYU Studies is the leading scholarly publication that focuses on LDS topics. It covers a variety of topics with articles that are well researched, written and edited. I read it all the time and highly recommend it.

Description from BOMC:

"BYU Studies is dedicated to publishing scholarly religious literature in the form of books, journals, and dissertations that is qualified, significant, and inspiring. We want to share these publications to help promote faith, continued learning, and further interest in our LDS history with those in the world who have a positive interest in this work. Throughout its history, the journal has published landmark articles in Book of Mormon research, and provides Book of Mormon resources for continued study, which can be found at http://byustudies.byu.edu/book-of-mormon-charts.

For the most part, *BYU Studies* avoids the topic of Book of Mormon geography. Two exceptions reflect full-blown Mesomania. One was the 2005 Library of Congress symposium discussed above. The other is section 13 of the charts in the link above. They all focus on Mesoamerica and never mention alternatives.

Chapter 17 – BYU Religious Studies Center

I refer to RSC publications often. I highly recommend this source on a variety of topics. You'll find some material that touches on Cumorah and Mesoamerica, but RSC does an excellent job with balance and objectivity.

Description from BOMC:

"The Religious Studies Center is a vital research and publications arm of Religious Education. It exists to seek out, encourage, and publish faithful gospel scholarship through sponsoring symposia and seminars; awarding research grants; and producing and disseminating high quality, peer-reviewed works. These include monographs, journals, compilations, and other publications in print and electronic formats pertaining to the content and context of Latter-day Saint scripture, the doctrines and history of the Restoration, and the restored Church including its relationship to other cultures, religions, and the behavioral sciences. The RSC's Book of Mormon publications have been invaluable to the furthering of Book of Mormon research."

Chapter 18 – Interpreter

I can't recommend the *Interpreter*. If you like Mesomania, read the *Interpreter*.

In my opinion, the name reflects the editorial stance; i.e., you have a group of scholars that think they should interpret the scriptures for others.

There are some excellent, thoughtful articles, but also some agenda-driven articles that, in my opinion, are not peer reviewed but peer approved. In some respects, the *Interpreter* represents the worst of the old FARMS.

BOMC description:

"The Interpreter Foundation is a nonprofit educational organization focused on the scriptures of The Church of Jesus Christ of Latter-day Saints: the Book of Mormon, the Pearl of Great Price, the Bible, the Doctrine and Covenants, early LDS history, and related subjects. Their goal is to increase understanding of scripture through careful scholarly investigation and analysis of the insights provided by a wide range of ancillary disciplines, including language, history, archaeology, literature, culture, ethnohistory, art, geography, law, politics, philosophy, etc."

Chapter 19 – FairMormon

FairMormon is a sort of Mormon Wikipedia. They do a good job collecting sources and organizing them by topic. They also do a good job answering questions—for the most part.

But it's full-fledged Mesomania.

BOMC description: "Fair Mormon is an organization dedicated to apologetics and answering different questions on faith."

Although the authors are anonymous, Mesomania dominates the site. Every discussion of Book of Mormon geography and historicity reflects the consensus Mesomania.

Actually, it's worse than that. If you want to see a perfect example of Mesomania, go to the FairMormon site and search for Cumorah. There you'll find the list of 13 geographical conditions for Cumorah that include volcanoes and other criteria designed to exclude New York and point to Mesoamerica. You'll find the warning of Joseph Fielding Smith dismissed because of 50-year-old hearsay from a BYU student. You'll read that Joseph and Oliver never visited the repository but had a vision of a hill in Mexico. Etc.

Chapter 20 – More Good Foundation

This is an awesome resource. It focuses on action and I highly recommend it.

BOMC description:

"The More Good Foundation is a 501(c)(3) non-profit organization that helps Mormons share their beliefs on the Internet so interested people can learn more about Mormonism. It was created in 2005 by David Neeleman, founder of JetBlue Airways, and James Engebretsen, Associate Dean of the BYU Marriott School, as a solution to the overwhelming need for increased positive and accurate information about the LDS faith on the Internet. It is operated by a small team of employees and many volunteers."

The only caveat might be some of the links, such as Askgramps.org, which incorporates Mesomania in its answers about the Book of Mormon. But don't let that stop you from working with the More Good Foundation.

Chapter 21 – Ancient America Foundation

This is the organization behind Book of Mormon Central. The logo—a Mayan pyramid—depicts full Mesomania. The web page cycles photos from Mesoamerica and a map of the area.

BOMC description:

"Ancient America Foundation is a Utah-based 501 (c) 3 public charity organized in 1983. Ancient America Foundation is dedicated to serious Book of Mormon research. During the 1990's and 2000's, key people in AAF included Richard K. Miner, V. Garth Norman, and Bruce W. Warren. Kirk A. Magleby joined the organization as General Manager in 2010. That same year, AAF began funding projects managed by John W. (Jack) Welch. In 2015, major donors came forward and tasked AAF with a mission to revitalize Book of Mormon studies. AAF's principal initiative, Book of Mormon Central, was born with Jack Welch as chairman."

AAF is the successor to a series of organizations dedicated to Book of Mormon archaeology that all focused on Mesoamerica, so it's not a surprise that BOMC continues this tradition.

Mesomania

Chapter 22 – Book of Mormon Onomasticon

This is another wonderful resource that I use all the time. It reflects some Mesomania at times, but you shouldn't have a problem with that because it incorporates ideas from many cultures. Definitely, take a look at this one.

BOMC description:

"The Book of Mormon Onomasticon is a vast work that compiles possible etymologies and origins of all personal names mentioned in the Book of Mormon text. This initiative is dedicated to deciphering the linguistic roots of Book of Mormon names to show the anitquity of Book of Mormon personal names."

Chapter 23 – Chiasmus Resources and Scripture Citation Index

Both of these are helpful and worth taking a look. BOMC descriptions:

"Chiasmus Resources. This website is designed to help in the research and study of chiasmus, a literary device found in texts from many cultures, most notably in ancient texts. This website offers a vast bibliography of works on chiasmus, and also a continually growing index that provides references to chiasmus in scripture. The Chiasmus Index provides a sizeable collection of references to the Book of Mormon, which can be found at the link."

"Scripture Citation Index. The Scripture Citation Index, created by Stephen W. Liddle and Richard C. Galbraith, integrates all four standard works of the LDS Church with General Conference talks from 1942 to the present. All references to scripture in General Conference talks are linked to individual verses in the scriptures, so that as you read, you can refer to any sermon to ever refer to that scripture. The Index additionally integrates *Journal of Discourses*, *Teachings of the Prophet Joseph Smith*, and *Scriptural Teachings of the Prophet Joseph Smith*."

Chapter 24 – BMAF

BMAF (Book of Mormon Archaeological Forum) is 100% Mesomania. Basically, it's a club for Mesoamerican advocates.

Although BOMC does not list BMAF as an affiliate, BMAF is a division of BOMC. (I'm not sure what that means, other than it reinforces the Mesomania orientation of BOMC.)

Here's the BMAF mission statement, from http://www.bmaf.org/about/mission_statement.

"The Book of Mormon Archaeological Forum (BMAF) is a 501(c)(3) not for profit organization dedicated as an open forum for presentation, dissemination, and discussion of research and evidences regarding Book of Mormon archaeology, anthropology, geography and culture **within a Mesoamerican context.** Our goals are (1) to increase understanding of the Book of **Mormon as an ancient Mesoamerican document,** (2) to correlate and publish works of LDS scholars, (3) to help promote unity and cooperation among scholars and students of the Book of Mormon, and (4) to provide a forum where responsible scholars can present current ideas and discoveries."

Chapter 25 –Maxwell Institute/ FARMS

Although it is not listed as an affiliate of BOMC, the BOMC database contains material published by the Maxwell Institute/FARMS.

Whether or not it started that way, FARMS became 100% Mesomania. It was absorbed into the Maxwell Institute at BYU, which means the Maxwell Institute hosts the FARMS publications on its website.

According to Wikipedia, "The Foundation for Ancient Research and Mormon Studies (FARMS) was an informal collaboration of academics devoted to Latter-day Saint historical scholarship. In 1997, the group became a formal part of Brigham Young University (BYU). In 2006, the group became a formal part of the Neal A. Maxwell Institute for Religious Scholarship, formerly known as the Institute for the Study and Preservation of Ancient Religious Texts, BYU. BYU is owned and operated by The Church of Jesus Christ of Latter-day Saints (LDS Church). FARMS has since been absorbed into the Maxwell Institute's Laura F. Willes Center for Book of Mormon Studies."

Mesomania

"FARMS supported and sponsored what it considered to be "faithful scholarship", which includes academic study and research in support of Christianity and Mormonism, and in particular, the official position of the LDS Church. This research primarily concerned the Book of Mormon, the Book of Abraham, the Old Testament, the New Testament, early Christian history, ancient temples, and other related subjects. While allowing some degree of academic freedom to its scholars, FARMS was committed to the conclusion that LDS scriptures are authentic, historical texts written by prophets of God. FARMS has been criticized by scholars and critics who classify it as an apologetics organization that operated under the auspices of the LDS Church."

In my view, the early-stage FARMS produced many important publications dealing with the Book of Mormon and other topics. Over time, the organization became more focused on polemics.

The old FARMS material is part of the scholarly record, so it is widely available. I think that's unfortunate. Recently an investigator sent me some FARMS material to explain why he can't accept the Book of Mormon.

I'd love to see the Maxwell Institute repudiate the old FARMS stuff, but I don't think that will ever happen.

Chapter 26 – LDS Scholars

You may have noticed by now that I've avoided naming specific living individuals. Where it was necessary to include citations, I made them endnotes.

Why don't I identify the scholars by name?

Because I don't think it matters *who* wrote *what* about Mesomania (except for Joseph Fielding Smith).

Mesomania is pretty much universal by now, so there's no reason to name names. That looks like assigning blame, and I don't blame anyone for Mesomania.

We all inherited it.

As I wrote at the outset, some of us are more resistant than others, and some are more susceptible than others.

Besides, on a personal level I like and respect everyone who engages in Book of Mormon research. That doesn't mean I agree with everyone, but I wouldn't want criticism to be taken personally by any individual, and I wouldn't want readers to think I don't respect the work of any of these scholars.

We have all benefited from their research and writing on many topics related to the Book of Mormon. On geography, however, in my view they have relied on two premises they should not have.

First, they reject what Oliver Cowdery, David Whitmer and others said about the Hill Cumorah.

Second, they rely on the anonymous 1842 *Times and Seasons* articles.

As useful as scholarly contributions can be, you don't have to defer to anyone on this topic of Book of Mormon geography. The main issues are simple, clear, and easy to understand.

As are the cures for Mesomania.

Section C: Five Cures

Whether you were born into the Church or joined later in life, you have been exposed to Mesomania. It's unavoidable.

It's so pervasive that people don't even realize that's what they're looking at when they look at the paintings on chapel walls, or in the Gospel Art collection.

But before we discuss cures, we need to know where we stand.

Two things people hate:

1. The way things are.
2. Change.

If you don't like the way things are and you seek a cure for Mesomania, then move ahead to Chapter 27. I'm going to take a moment for those who are satisfied with the way things are and don't want to change.

Maybe you don't mind the way things are because you're comfortable with Mesomania. As I've said all along, that's perfectly fine. It's okay to have different ideas. In that case, all I ask is that you recognize the implications. You're in the water and you're comfortable, but a lot of people around you—and even more people who aren't in the water—recognize that the two-Cumorahs theory does cause people to be confused and disturbed in their faith. They are uncomfortable with the idea that Oliver Cowdery and David Whitmer were misleading people about the Hill Cumorah, for example, or that Joseph Smith passively adopted a false tradition about Cumorah.

So by all means, stay in the Mesomania water. But don't be surprised when others step out—or refuse to get in—because they see it's a mirage.

Maybe you don't like the way things are but you're afraid of change because you think you're being disloyal to what you've been taught your entire life.

But what have you *really* been taught?

Probably that Joseph Smith was a prophet, that the Book of Mormon is true, and that the Three Witnesses are reliable and truthful.

Probably not that Friberg painted accurate scenes.

Trust the Prophet. Trust the text. Trust the Three Witnesses.

Most of all, trust yourself.

Chapter 27 – Letter VII

Looking back, it was obvious and clear from the earliest days of the Church.

The Hill Cumorah is in New York.

In this book I've tried to show how that simple fact became obscured. Mesomania is both the cause and the result.

The first cure, in my opinion, is Letter VII.

Oliver wrote this with Joseph's help. We have the Assistant President of the Church and the President of the Church collaborating to tell the world about the early events in Church history.

Not only did they tell it, but Joseph put it in his journal as part of his story, and saw that it was republished multiple times.

But if you're like most members of the Church in 2016, you haven't read Letter VII.

You probably haven't even heard about it.

So definitely, read it soon. Today. Now.

The Church history letters Oliver wrote with Joseph's assistance include detailed information about Moroni's first visit to Joseph, including his appearance.

Mesomania

One key point: Moroni told Joseph the record was *written* and *deposited* not far from that place," meaning where Joseph lived.

Mormon wrote most of the record. Moroni finished it up. So if the record was written near Joseph's home, Mormon and Moroni both lived in New York.

Which is what we expect when we realize the Hill Cumorah is in New York.

Once we have Letter VII in mind, we're ready to understand a lot more about Church history. Now it makes sense that Joseph and Oliver visited the repository in the Hill Cumorah. It makes sense that during Joseph's lifetime, and during the lifetime of everyone who knew him, no one questioned the New York setting for the Hill Cumorah.

And yet, Mesomania is persistent. The force is strong with this one. So we have to consider additional factors.

Chapter 28 – Plains, Zelph, and Indians

To paraphrase Isaac Newton, for every argument there is an equal and opposite argument.

Except maybe not equal.

We've discussed what Joseph Smith said about the plains of the Nephites, Zelph, and the Indians living in this country. Learn all you can about these events.

These all appear straightforward and clear, but when viewed through the Mesomania lens, they look much different.

In Appendix 1, you can compare the two perspectives for yourself. See what you think.

The best explanation, speaking from the Mesomania perspective, is that Joseph recognized Nephite elements who lived in the hinterlands; i.e., Nephites who had migrated northward and retained enough of their culture and identity that Joseph recognized it when he saw it.

The worst Mesomania explanation is that Joseph was a clueless speculator.

But without doubt, the simplest explanation is that Joseph knew what he was talking about.

Chapter 29 – Archaeology, Geology, etc.

Truth is truth, so we expect the sciences to validate, or at least corroborate, the Book of Mormon.

The first step, of course, is to understand what the text actually says.

Mesomania sets up expectations designed to direct us to a pre-determined area, such as the requirement that the Nephites lived among active volcanos. We'll discuss the expectation problem in the next chapter.

The sciences are a cure for Mesomania because when we look at North America, we can find corroboration for what the text actually says.

You can delve as deeply as you want in the sciences, but you don't have to be a geologist to read about the New Madrid earthquakes in Missouri and see how closely they describe conditions such as those in 3 Nephi 8.

You don't have to be an archaeologist to learn about the thousands of earthworks in North America that corroborate what the Nephites said about their construction methods.

Bottom line: embrace the sciences, but first recognize what your expectations are.

Chapter 30 – Expectations from the text

A core principle of Mesomania is that the text of the Book of Mormon takes precedence over any other source. In case of a conflict, the text prevails.

The text takes precedence over the Doctrine and Covenants, the Pearl of Great Price, and statements of Joseph Smith, Oliver Cowdery, and any of their associates.

In theory, this makes sense. We would probably all agree.

But in practice, this Mesomania tenet actually means that the *interpretation* of the text—particularly the interpretation by select scholars—takes precedence.

If you think this all sounds like academic or legal technicalities, you're correct.

But the text is an important cure.

When you look at a Friberg painting or read an article or book inspired by Mesomania, double-check the text. If you don't already know, you'll discover the text never mentions jungles, volcanoes, pyramids, jaguars, jade, tapirs, or other basic features of life in ancient Mesoamerica. It doesn't even mention mountains until you get to Helaman.

There is not a single reference to a stone building anywhere in the text. Even when a small group of dissenters used cement, they used it only to build houses, and they used it with wood, not stone.

A good example of non-textual expectations is the requirement, so often repeated in Mesomania literature, that the Nephites lived among volcanoes.

The text never mentions volcanoes, which is surprising, since the people supposedly lived among active volcanoes for 1,000 years.

But people wearing the Mesomania lens see volcanoes in the text and therefore require that any proposed geography feature volcanoes.

When you read a list of requirements produced by Mesomania, go back to the text and see if these requirements are really there, or if they simply reflect what people see through the Mesomania lens.[17]

Mesomania also causes people to find similarities, or correspondences, between the text and Mayan culture. The argument goes like this: Nephites had farms. Mayans had farms. Therefore, Nephites were Mayans.

Whenever you see a Mesomania discussion of correspondences, ask yourself if this is a specific feature or if it's common to most human cultures.

Mesomania

Chapter 31 – Moroni's America

To reiterate a key point: there are two categories of Book of Mormon geography theories:

1. Cumorah is in New York.
2. Cumorah is somewhere else.

For me, if you don't put Cumorah in New York, it doesn't matter where you put it. You're rejecting Oliver Cowdery and Joseph Smith in favor of your preferred interpretation of the text.

Again, if you're comfortable with that, and you're still in the water—still committed to the Book of Mormon—that's fine.

But in a real world framework, people want to know how the rest of the Book of Mormon fits with Cumorah in New York.

You guessed it. I have an idea.

Cumorah is the end of the line. Everything written about the Jaredites and the Nephites leads up to Cumorah.

There's nothing after Cumorah.

So when we put a pin in the map of New York for Cumorah, where did everything else take place?

Let's imagine we have a compass. We put the point on top of the Hill Cumorah in New York and then pull the arm away from the point. Should we go 10 miles? 100? 1,000? 5,000?

This is where the interpretation comes into play.

At one extreme, I've seen proposed geographies that put the entire Book of Mormon in New York State. At the other, we have Orson Pratt putting Lehi's landing site in Chile.

A big range of possibilities.

Overall, though, I think most readers agree with the scholars who say the text describes an area of about 800 miles in diameter (assuming a circle).

For what it's worth, I generally agree the diameter wouldn't be more than 1,000 miles.

As an experiment, I relied on D&C 125 to put another pin in the map for Zarahemla.

Distance: about 850 miles.

From there, I went through the text from 1 Nephi 1 through Moroni 10 and found that the text describes North America quite well.

My book is *Moroni's America*. There's a full version and a pocket edition, as well as a web page.

I think it's a great cure for Mesomania, but I'm not saying it's the only one. I'd love to have someone come up with a better idea. Maybe you will.

Chapter 32 – Looking Forward

The Book of Helaman tells us what happened in Nephite society in the years leading up to the first coming of the Lord.

It parallels events leading up to the second coming.

Chapter 3 describes a sequence of events that reflect what is happening in our day.

The chapter starts out with no contention among the people, except for a little pride in the church that caused some "little dissensions among the people, which affairs were settled in the ending of the forty and third year."

We can compare that to the early days of the Church, when "some little dissensions" led people to oppose Joseph Smith and leave the Church. But the Church survived and thrived, for the most part, for over a hundred years. Not without challenges to overcome, but the progress of the Church was steady.

Then, verse 3 says in the forty and sixth year, "there was much contention and many dissensions." People left the church and the land of Zarahemla; "there were an exceedingly great many who departed."

Verse 17 says the people left "after there had been great contentions, and disturbances."

I think we can relate this to Book of Mormon geography and historicity. Joseph Fielding Smith even invoked this terminology when he said the two-Cumorahs theory caused members to become *disturbed* in their faith.

Notice the contention continued for a few years, but then they "began to cease" in the latter end of the forty and eighth year. In the forty and ninth year, there was continual peace.

Verse 24: "And it came to pass that in this same year there was exceedingly great prosperity in the church, insomuch that there were thousands who did join themselves unto the church and were baptized unto repentance."

Now, look at what happened as a result of eliminating the contention:

25. "And so great was the prosperity of the church, and so many the blessings which were poured out upon the people, that *even the high priests and the teachers were themselves astonished beyond measure.*"

I think this is what will happen as members of the Church eliminate contention about Book of Mormon geography and reach unity on the basic teaching from Oliver and Joseph that the Hill Cumorah was in New York.

Chapter 33 – Executive Summary

Here are 13 take-aways from this book:

1. Joseph Smith and Oliver Cowdery told the world exactly where the Hill Cumorah is—in upstate New York, a few miles south of Palmyra.

2. The location of Cumorah was never questioned during Joseph's lifetime—or during the lifetime of any of his associates.

3. Everything directly attributable to Joseph Smith placed the Book of Mormon in North America—specifically, the United States circa 1842.

4. Nothing that links the Book of Mormon to Central or South American can be directly attributed to Joseph Smith.

5. In the 1920s, RLDS scholars proposed that all Book of Mormon events took place in a limited area of Central America; i.e., Cumorah was not in New York. They developed a "two-Cumorahs" theory whereby the *real* Cumorah—the scene of the final battles and Mormon's repository (Mormon 6:6)—was in Central America. The hill in New York was merely the place where Moroni buried the abridged plates. It had no name. Unknown early Mormons called it Cumorah and the name stuck, but it was a mistake.

6. LDS scholars picked up the RLDS theory.

7. In 1936, Joseph Fielding Smith (JFS), Church Historian and a 20-year member of the Quorum of the Twelve, denounced the two-Cumorah theory and said **"because of this theory some members of the Church have become confused and greatly disturbed in their faith in the Book of Mormon."**

8. LDS scholars ignored JFS and pursued decades of study intended to verify the Mesoamerican setting.

9. In the 1950s, JFS, now President of the Quorum of the Twelve, reiterated his warning in *Doctrines of Salvation*. Again, he was ignored.

10. In the 1950s, Arnold Friberg created the famous Book of Mormon paintings depicting Central America. They have become ubiquitous, published in millions of copies of missionary and foreign language editions of the text, displayed on the walls of Church buildings, and published in Church magazines.

11. The Mesoamerican theory became the consensus view of LDS scholars and educators, supported by Church media. Mesomania ruled.

12. As JFS warned, the Mesoamerican theory has caused members to become confused and disturbed in their faith. It is prominent in anti-Mormon literature.

13. New research into Church history clarifies what Joseph and Oliver taught. Modern science—and the text itself—show that Joseph and Oliver were right all along.

Appendix I: Agree/Disagree Tables

Because so many books and articles have been written, it is difficult to sort through the various positions taken by advocates of various theories.

As discussed in this book, there are two basic positions regarding Cumorah: either it was in New York, or it was elsewhere.

I have simplified the analysis below to compare two proposed geographies that I am most familiar with; i.e., Mesoamerica and Moroni's America. There are variations on each, but the basic premises of each camp are the same because the distinction has to do with the location of Cumorah.

The table sets out areas of agreement and areas in which the two sides agree to disagree.

As you will see, there are far more areas of agreement than disagreement, which suggests more unity than is sometimes conveyed by the various writings.

I intend this to be an accurate representation. I'm always open to correction and editing if anyone has useful suggestions to make.

The tables are arranged on facing pages. Each box is numbered for convenience.

Mesomania

Book of Mormon message
1. The most important aspect of the Book of Mormon is its message.
2. The Book of Mormon is an inspired translation of an actual ancient record of actual people who lived in the real world.
3. The ultimate objective of our research/writing is to motivate people to read the Book of Mormon and strengthen their faith in Christ as a result.
4. Another objective of our research/writing is to help people better understand the text of the book by understanding its setting, culture and context.

Church Position
5. The Church has no official position on where Book of Mormon events took place.
6. As an Apostle and Church Historian, Joseph Fielding Smith said the two-Cumorahs theory caused members to become confused and disturbed in their faith in the Book of Mormon. He reiterated this when he was President of the Quorum of the Twelve in the 1950s in his book *Doctrines of Salvation*.
7. Joseph Fielding Smith's comments on the two-Cumorahs theory…

	Book of Mormon message	
	Mesoamerica	Moroni's America
1.	Agree	Agree
2.	Agree	Agree
3.	Agree	Agree
4.	Agree	Agree

	Church Position	
	Mesoamerica	Moroni's America
5.	Agree	Agree
6.	Agree	Agree
7.	Joseph Fielding Smith's criticisms of the two-Cumorahs theory are **invalid** because he did not know much about Mesoamerica and because 50 years ago, someone heard a BYU professor say Pres. Smith told him he could teach whatever he wanted about Cumorah	Joseph Fielding Smith's criticisms of the two-Cumorahs theory are **valid**, have caused and continue to cause members to become confused and disturbed in their faith of the Book of Mormon.

Church Position
8. Modern prophets/apostles have identified Lamanites in Latin America.

Hill Cumorah
9. In Letter VII, Oliver Cowdery identified the valley west of the Hill Cumorah in New York as the location of the final battles of the Nephites and Jaredites.
10. Joseph Smith instructed his scribes to copy Oliver's letters, including Letter VII, into his journal as part of his life story.
11. Joseph Smith gave permission to Benjamin Winchester to republish Oliver's letters, including Letter VII, in his newspaper called the *Gospel Reflector*
12. Don Carlos republished Oliver's letters, including Letter VII, in the 1842 Church newspaper called the *Times and Seasons* (T&S).
13. Reliability of Letter VII.

	Church Position	
	Mesoamerica	Moroni's America
8.	These statements corroborate the Mesoamerican setting that Nephites and Lamanites lived in Mesoamerica.	These statements are not limited to Mesoamerica and reflect post-Book of Mormon migrations (Mayans moving north after 800 AD, intermarrying, and then returning to Mesoamerica and south from there).

	Hill Cumorah	
	Mesoamerica	Moroni's America
9.	Agree	Agree
10.	Agree	Agree
11.	Agree	Agree
12.	Agree	Agree
13.	Oliver Cowdery was speculating and was factually wrong about the New York location of the Hill Cumorah.	Oliver Cowdery stated a fact about the New York Cumorah based on his own experience in Mormon's repository as related to Brigham Young and others.

Hill Cumorah
14. Joseph Smith originally obtained the plates from a stone box Moroni constructed out of stone and cement in the Hill Cumorah in New York.
15. Lucy Mack Smith wrote "'Stop, father, stop,' said Joseph, 'it was the angel of the Lord. As I passed by the hill of Cumorah, where the plates are, the angel met me and said that I had not been engaged enough in the work of the Lord; that the time had come for the record to be brought forth.'" (Lucy Mack Smith, History of Joseph Smith by His Mother, 1853).
16. Brigham Young said Oliver told him that he (Oliver) and Joseph had made at least two visits to a room in the Hill Cumorah in New York that contained piles of records and ancient Nephite artifacts.
17. Mormon said he buried all the Nephite records in the Hill Cumorah (Morm. 6:6), the scene of the final battles of the Nephites, except he kept out the plates he gave to his son Moroni to finish the record.
18. The location of the Hill Cumorah (the site of the final battles of the Jaredites and of the Nephites.
19. One Cumorah vs. the two-Cumorahs theory.

	Hill Cumorah	
	Mesoamerica	Moroni's America
14.	Agree	Agree
15.	Agree	Agree
16.	Agree	Agree
17.	Agree	Agree
18.	The hill in New York had nothing to do with ancient Nephites or Jaredites (apart from Moroni traveling to the area). The real Hill Cumorah which contains Mormon's repository of records and was the scene of the final battles is elsewhere.	The hill in New York is the actual Hill Cumorah/Ramah where both the Nephites and the Jaredites were destroyed. It also contained Mormon's repository of the Nephite records.
19.	There are two Cumorahs. Moroni buried the plates in the New York hill. Unknown early Mormons named this hill Cumorah and Joseph Smith later adopted this tradition. The real Cumorah where Mormon deposited the Nephite records is the scene of the final battles and it is in Mesoamerica.	There is only one Cumorah and it is in New York. Mormon's record repository and Moroni's stone box were both in this hill, but in different locations.

Mesomania

Hill Cumorah
20. Meaning of D&C 128:20: "And again, what do we hear? Glad tidings from Cumorah! Moroni, an angel from heaven, declaring the fulfilment of the prophets—the book to be revealed," followed by references to other events that took place in New York.

Church History: Joseph's knowledge
21. Joseph Smith obtained the plates from Moroni from the hill near his house now called Cumorah.
22. Joseph's mother wrote that "During our evening conversations, Joseph would occasionally … describe the ancient inhabitants of this continent, their dress, mode of travelings, and the animals upon which they rode; their cities, their buildings, with every particular; their mode of warfare; and also their religious worship. This he would do with as much ease, seemingly, as if he had spent his whole life among them."
23. In the Wentworth letter, Joseph wrote "I was also informed concerning the aboriginal inhabitants of this country and shown who they were, and from whence they came; a brief sketch of their origin, progress, civilization, laws, governments, of their righteousness and iniquity, and the blessings of God being finally withdrawn from them as a people, was [also] made known unto me; I was also told where were deposited some plates on which were engraven an abridgment of the records of the ancient prophets that had existed on this continent.

	Hill Cumorah	
	Mesoamerica	Moroni's America
20.	Joseph was either embracing a folk tradition started by an unknown member or was paying homage to the real Cumorah in Mexico.	Joseph was referring to the hill in New York that was referred to as Cumorah by Moroni.

	Church History: Joseph's knowledge	
	Mesoamerica	Moroni's America
21.	Agree	Agree
22.	Agree	Agree
23.	Agree	Agree

Church History: Joseph's knowledge
24. Joseph Smith's general knowledge about Book of Mormon geography.
25. "Plains of the Nephites." During the Zion's Camp march, while in Illinois on the banks of the Mississippi, Joseph wrote a letter to Emma. The camp had just crossed Indiana and Ohio. Joseph wrote, "The whole of our journey, in the midst of so large a company of social honest and sincere men, **wandering over the plains of the Nephites**, recounting occasionally the history of the Book of Mormon, roving over the mounds of that once beloved people of the Lord, picking up their skulls and their bones, as a proof of its divine authenticity,"
26. Zelph. At a site in Illinois during Zion's Camp, Wilford Woodruff wrote, "While on our travels we visited many of the mounds which were flung up by the ancient inhabitants of this continent probably by the Nephites & Lamanites. … We visited one of those Mounds…. Elder Milton Holmes took the arrow out of the back bones that killed Zelph & brought it with some of the bones in to the camp… Brother Joseph had a vission respecting the person. He said he was a white Lamanite. The curs was taken from him or at least in part. He was killed in battle with an arrow. The arrow was found among his ribs. One of his thigh bones was broken. This was done by a stone flung from a sling in battle years before his death. His name was Zelph. Zelph was a large thick set man and a man of God. He was a warrior under the great prophet /Onandagus/ that was known from the hill Camorah /or east sea/ to the Rocky mountains. The above knowledge Joseph receieved in a vision." The arrowhead is said to be in Church archives today.

	Church History: Joseph's knowledge	
	Mesoamerica	Moroni's America
24.	Joseph did not leave a first-hand record of a revelation about Book of Mormon geography, so he had no revelation or inspiration regarding Book of Mormon geography	Joseph Smith knew where the Book of Mormon events took place because Moroni had shown him, as mentioned in the Wentworth letter and by his mother Lucy.
25.	Joseph speculated about a location not specifically mentioned in the text ("the plains of the Nephites"). The Midwestern U.S. is part of the "Hinterlands." This is where Nephites migrated northward, but not part of the text.	Joseph recognized the plains referred to in the Book of Mormon; i.e., "meet them upon the plains between the two cities" (Alma 52:20); "pitch their tents in the plains of Nephihah" (Alma 62:18) and "battle against them, upon the plains" (Alma 62:19).
26.	Zelph was a warrior killed in Illinois who was known to some of Lehi's descendants who migrated northward from Mesoamerica into the Hinterlands.	Zelph was a warrior in the final battles of the Nephites, killed in Illinois between Zarahemla and Cumorah. (Zelph's mound is 100 miles southeast of Nauvoo/Zarahemla.)

Mesomania

Church History: Joseph's knowledge
27. 1830-31 Mission to the Lamanites by Oliver Cowdery, Ziba Peterson, Parley P. Pratt, and Peter Whitmer, Jr. (D&C 28, 30 and 32)
28. Statements attributed to Joseph Smith were recorded years after the fact by Wilford Woodruff and Martha Coray and say that Zion is all of North and South America

Church History: Bernhisel and the Stephens books
29. On Sept. 9, 1841, Dr. Bernhisel gave Wilford Woodruff a copy of John Lloyd Stephens' popular two-volume set of books titled Incidents of Travel in Central America, Chiapas, and Yucatan to give to Joseph Smith.
30. On his trip to Nauvoo, Woodruff read the Stephens books.
31. On Nov. 5, 1841, Wilford Woodruff wrote a letter to Dr. Bernhisel that is not extant.

	Church History: Joseph's knowledge	
	Mesoamerica	Moroni's America
27.	Early Mormons believed the American Indians were Lamanites, but the term actually refers to all indigenous people in the Americas.	These verses identified the tribes visited in New York, Ohio and Missouri, showing these tribes are the descendants of the Lamanites.
28.	These statements mean Lehi's descendants filled the hemisphere, but the Book of Mormon events took place in a limited geography (Mesoamerica).	These statements originally meant Northern and Southern States, not continents. Winchester's wing concept (Isa. 18:1) about the continents was adopted by Hyrum Smith, then applied retroactively by Wilford Woodruff and Martha Coray.

	Church History: Bernhisel and the Stephens books	
	Mesoamerica	Moroni's America
29.	Agree	Agree
30.	Agree	Agree
31.	Agree	Agree

Church History: Bernhisel and the Stephens books
32. A thank-you letter dated Nov. 16, 1841, written to Bernhisel on Joseph Smith's behalf, was mailed several days later. No one knows who wrote the letter because the handwriting remains unidentified and no journals mention it.
33. Several long extracts from the Stephens books were published in the 1842 *Times and Seasons* with editorial comments linking the Book of Mormon to Central America.
34. Wilford Woodruff purchased additional copies of the Stephens books for John Taylor and wrote about them several times in his journal.
35. Joseph donated copies of the Stephens books to the Nauvoo Library in 1844.
36. Significance of Bernhisel letter.

Church History: the *Times and Seasons (T&S)*
37. From February 15 through October 15, 1842, the boilerplate of the T&S said the paper was edited, printed, and published by Joseph Smith.
38. A series of editorials in the T&S during 1842 linked the Book of Mormon to archaeological findings in North and Central America, citing *American Antiquities*, an archaeology book by Josiah Priest. All were published either anonymously or over the signature of Ed. for Editor.

	Church History: Bernhisel and the Stephens books	
	Mesoamerica	Moroni's America
32.	Agree	Agree
33.	Agree	Agree
34.	Agree	Agree
35.	Agree	Agree
36.	Because the Bernhisel letter was written on behalf of Joseph Smith, he dictated it or knew of and approved its contents. This means he enthusiastically embraced the discoveries in Central America as evidence of the Book of Mormon.	Joseph often had others write on his behalf. The Bernhisel letter was drafted by Wilford Woodruff and written out by an unknown person with good penmanship. Joseph probably asked Woodruff to write the letter but never saw it and never read the Stephens books.

	Church History: the *Times and Seasons (T&S)*	
	Mesoamerica	Moroni's America
37.	Agree	Agree
38.	Agree	Agree

Mesomania

Church History: the *Times and Seasons (T&S)*
39. Anonymous T&S articles, published in Sept/Oct 1842, contained long extracts from the Stephens books and claimed Zarahemla was in Quirigua, Guatemala, and that Lehi "landed a little south of the Isthmus of Darien."
40. In March 1842, T&S published Joseph Smith's letter to Mr. Wentworth, who lived in Chicago, Illinois. He wrote, "The remnant [of Book of Mormon peoples] are the Indians that now inhabit this country."
41. Significance of T&S boilerplate listing Joseph Smith as printer, editor and publisher of T&S.
42. Significance of the anonymous Sept/Oct Stephens articles.
43. Significance of the Wentworth letter sentence that the remnant are the Indians that now inhabit this country.

Tribes

Mesomania

	Church History: the *Times and Seasons* (*T&S*)	
	Mesoamerica	Moroni's America
39.	Agree	Agree
40.	Agree	Agree
41.	Joseph was a hands-on editor of the T&S who wrote or approved of all the anonymous articles as well as all the articles signed by "ED."	Joseph was a nominal editor only who probably never even read the paper until after it was published. The paper was actually edited by William Smith and/or W.W. Phelps, and most unattributed material came through the mail.
42.	The Sept/Oct articles were written, or approved by, Joseph Smith. They show he didn't know where the Book of Mormon took place and was open to Central America.	Joseph had nothing to do with the Sept/Oct articles, which were written by Winchester and edited by William Smith and/or W.W. Phelps. Joseph resigned after these articles were published.
43.	The sentence refers to all indigenous people in the Western Hemisphere.	Joseph and Mr. Wentworth both lived in Illinois, so the sentence refers to the Native American Indians in Illinois and what was then the United States.

Mesomania

Book of Mormon geography
44. The geography passages in the Book of Mormon are subject to a variety of interpretations.
45. To date, apart from Moroni's stone box, the plates and other objects Joseph Smith showed to the Witnesses, and Zelph's mound, no artifact or archaeological site that can be directly linked to the Book of Mormon has been found anywhere.
46. Cultural characteristics can be discerned from the text.
47. The land of Zarahemla is north of the land of Nephi and lower in elevation than the land of Nephi.
48. The New Jerusalem Ether wrote about is located in Jackson County, Missouri.
49. Book of Mormon overall geography shape is… Awesome
50. Using the text to fit the described geography in a real-world setting results in a setting in…
51. The location of the city of Zarahemla is…

Mesomania

| | Book of Mormon geography ||
	Mesoamerica	Moroni's America
44.	Agree	Agree
45.	Agree	Agree
46.	Agree	Agree
47.	Agree	Agree
48.	Agree	Agree
49.	The text describes an overall hourglass shape. The narrow neck of land is in Central America. The locations of Cumorah and Zarahemla are unknown.	The text does not describe an overall hourglass shape. The narrow neck of land is in Ether 10:20; i.e., it's a small feature now known as Niagara. Cumorah is in New York and Zarahemla is in Iowa.
50.	Central America, including Guatemala and Mexico.	North America, from Florida to New York and west to Missouri and Iowa.
51.	The City of Zarahemla is located somewhere in Mexico or Guatemala; D&C 125:3 does not refer to the Nephite Zarahemla.	The City of Zarahemla is located across from Nauvoo as indicated by D&C 125:3 (near Montrose Iowa).

Mesomania

52. The River Sidon flows north or south.

Archaeology and Anthropology
53. Pre-Classic Mayan civilization was well-developed around 600 B.C.
54. Mayan civilization collapsed around 800 A.D. and Mayans migrated to North America, where they lived for several hundred years before returning to Central America.
55. The Newark Ohio earthworks are the largest earthworks in the world and demonstrate knowledge of astronomy and geometry.
56. There were a million ancient mounds in North America before the Europeans arrived.
57. There have been around two million ancient skeletons buried in mounds in Illinois alone.
58. Cultural elements in the text relate to real-world cultures.

52.	Because the land of Nephi is south of the land of Zarahemla and people travel down to the land of Zarahemla from Nephi, and because the river Sidon flows past the city of Zarahemla, the River Sidon flows north. Sidon is the Umacita or Grijalva river in Mesoamerica.	Because the land of Nephi is south of the land of Zarahemla and people travel down to the land of Zarahemla from Nephi, the river between the two lands flows North. This is the Tennessee River, unnamed in the text. The text says that the river Sidon flows past the city of Zarahemla and along the land of Zarahemla, but not that it goes to the land of Nephi. Sidon is the upper Mississippi River.

	Archaeology and Anthropology	
	Mesoamerica	Moroni's America
53.	Agree	Agree
54.	Agree	Agree
55.	Agree	Agree
56.	Agree	Agree
57.	Agree	Agree
58.	Agree	Agree

Archaeology and Anthropology
59. Cultural elements in the text describe....
60. Correspondences in Central America between BoM and ancient cultures…
61. The Jaredites…
62. Presence of ancient writing is…

Mesomania

	Archaeology and Anthropology	
	Mesoamerica	Moroni's America
59.	an ancient Mesoamerican culture. Towers in the text refer to massive stone pyramids. Horses may be tapirs. The Nephites sacrificed agouti or other large rodents.	The text describes an ancient North American culture. Towers in the text refer to wooden towers. Horses are horses. The Nephites strictly observed the Law of Moses, including species.
60.	suggest the BoM took place in Central America, including Mayan banners, pyramids, stone temples, warfare, symbols of the tree of life, state-level society, etc.	are typical of most cultures and, to the extent they are unique to BoM, they reflect culture brought to Central America from North America when the Mayans returned after 900 AD.
61.	lived in Central America and were destroyed at the Hill Cumorah (Ramah) in Mexico.	expanded throughout the western hemisphere. Ether wrote only about his direct ancestors who lived in "this north country" and were destroyed at Cumorah in New York.
62.	required by the text and ancient writing systems are found only in Mesoamerica.	not required by the text because the Lamanites sought to destroy the records.

Archaeology and Anthropology
63. Archaeological evidence in North America of ancient cultures during Book of Mormon time frames…
64. DNA evidence.
65. Promised land covenant.
66. Uto-Aztecan languages have Hebrew and Egyptian influence, showing transoceanic interaction with Indians in western U.S. and Mexico.

	Archaeology and Anthropology	
	Mesoamerica	Moroni's America
63.	shows a tribal level society, but BoM describes a state-level society (monumental architecture, class structure).	shows a primarily tribal level society but also a long-lost state-level society with monumental architecture, just as BoM describes.
64.	All known DNA in Mesoamerica is Asian in origin, but DNA evidence is inconclusive; it cannot prove or disprove the Book of Mormon.	Northeastern (Great Lakes) Indian tribes have X2 haplotype (Middle-Eastern) but dating remains an open issue because scientists currently say the X2 haplotype appeared in the Great Lakes region thousands of years before Lehi (and Adam).
65.	Promised land and covenant land includes entire Western hemisphere.	Promised land and covenant land refers to the United States.
66.	Relevant to Mayan culture which bordered on these areas.	Uto-Aztecan is not Mayan. Algonquin (Great Lakes Indians) languages also have Hebrew and Egyptian influence.

Mesomania

Appendix II: Cumorah and Book of Mormon Geography

The fact that Cumorah is in New York eliminates Central America as a plausible setting for the Book of Mormon. The distances are just too far. Believers have to choose between a New York Cumorah and a Mesoamerican Cumorah. I hope this book makes that choice easier.

With Cumorah in New York, it's also easier to see how the text describes North America.

An in-depth discussion of geography is beyond the scope of this book, but here is an overview of the map that is discussed in more detail in *The Lost City of Zarahemla* and *Moroni's America*.

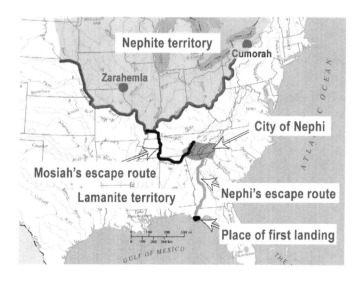

About the Author.

I contracted Mesomania at an early age. Like most Mormon kids, I was deeply impressed with the spectacular, full-color Arnold Friberg paintings in my large-print seminary edition of the Book of Mormon.

As a student at BYU, I took a class from John Sorenson. I studied books and articles published by FARMS and other LDS publishers. I visited sites in Central America, attended symposiums, and discussed the issues with a variety of experts.

But like many other people, both inside and outside the Church, I found the late-stage FARMS material increasingly unpersuasive. The scholars' pro-Mesoamerican arguments seemed to rely on sophistry and strained interpretations.

Then I learned about the Heartland geography model. I read Letter VII and was impressed by Oliver's confidence in the fact (as he put it) that Cumorah was in New York. I carefully examined the text and realized that what Mormon and Moroni were describing was *North America*—from New York to Missouri to Florida.

I recovered from Mesomania.
If you haven't already, I hope you do soon.

Jonathan Neville
September 2016

Mesomania

Endnotes

[1] Book of Mormon Archaeological Forum (bmaf.org), a division of Book of Mormon Central, a web page maintained by the Ancient America Foundation.

[2] John L. Sorenson, *Mormon's Codex* (Deseret Book and the Neal A. Maxwell Institute for Religious Scholarship at BYU, 2015), p. 688.

[3] Brant A. Gardner, *Traditions of the Fathers* (Greg Kofford Books), pp. 378-379

[4] Wilford Woodruff, letter to Parley P. Pratt, June 12, 1842, from Nauvoo, CHL, MS897_f0001_d0005_0001.jpg, available online at https://dcms.lds.org/delivery/DeliveryManagerServlet?dps_pid=IE1738096 (Woodruff letter to Pratt).

[5] For those interested, I dedicated an entire heavily annotated chapter to this letter in *Brought to Light*.

[6] For those interested in more detail, see *The Lost City of Zarahemla*, 2nd Edition, and *Brought to Light*.

[7] Boilerplate is term that refers to a block of type created as a single piece. In the early 1800s, printers had to set each character in place, a time-consuming task. Casting a block of type as a single piece saved a lot of time.

[8] Except one, when it was omitted for space reasons.

[9] Those interested can read *The Lost City of Zarahemla* and many other books and articles.

[10] Coincidentally, footnotes in the official 1879 LDS edition of the Book of Mormon that identified Cumorah in New York and speculated about South American locations were deleted in 1920.

[11] William J. Hamblin, quoted in Brant A. Gardner, "This Idea: The 'This Land' Series and the U.C.-Centric Reading of the Book of Mormon, FARMS Review 20/2 (2008): 141-62, online http://publications.mi.byu.edu/publications/review/20/2/S00007-5176a3c9e699d7Gardner.pdf

[12] More detail is available at http://bookofmormonwars.blogspot.com/2016/04/fun-with-david-palmer.html.

[13] More detail on this is available at http://bookofmormonwars.blogspot.com/2016/04/fun-with-john-e-clark-archaeology-and_17.html and http://bookofmormonwars.blogspot.com/2016/04/more-fun-with-brother-clark.html.

[14] Trent Toone, "Insight into Arnold Friberg's Book of Mormon paintings," *Deseret News*, May 21, 2012. Online at http://www.deseretnews.com/article/865556112/Insight-into-Arnold-Fribergs-Book-of-Mormon-paintings.html?pg=all.

[15] http://bookofmormonconsensus.blogspot.com/ has looked at several of the KnoWhys to show how they could have been improved by incorporating information and insights from the North American setting.

[16] https://bookofmormoncentral.org/content/affiliates

[17] I address expectation gaps in my blogs and web page, http://moronisamerica.com/